From
Rationality
to Liberation

From Rationality to Liberation

The Evolution of Feminist Ideology

Judith A. Sabrosky

CONTRIBUTIONS IN
POLITICAL SCIENCE, NUMBER 32

GREENWOOD PRESS
Westport, Connecticut • London England

Library of Congress Cataloging in Publication Data

Sabrosky, Judith A
    From rationality to liberation.

    (Contributions in political science ; no. 32
ISSN 0147-1066)
    Bibliography: p.
    Includes index.
    1. Feminism—History.   I.   Title.   II.   Series.
HQ1154.S135   1980   301.41'2'09   79-7065
ISBN 0-313-20672-4

Library of Congress Catalog Card Number: 79-7065
ISBN: 0-313-20672-4
ISSN: 0147-1066

First published in 1979

Greenwood Press, Inc.
51 Riverside Avenue, Westport, Connecticut 06880

Printed in the United States of America

10 9 8 7 6 5 4 3 2 1

To my family

Contents

Acknowledgments

THIS PROJECT ON FEMINIST ideology has been a long and often tedious one. As with most long projects, the debts accumulated in its pursuit are almost too numerous to mention. Yet several individual and institutional contributions were so important that they must be acknowledged. Patricia Kruppa, Herbert Hirsch, Armando Gutierrez, Carl Leiden, and especially David V. Edwards of the University of Texas at Austin provided insightful criticisms and valuable suggestions for improving an earlier version of the manuscript. The Foreign Policy Research Institute and Gallaudet College contributed invaluable secretarial and technical services. Discussions with the officers and cadets of the Department of Social Sciences at the United States Military Academy aided in refining many of the arguments and conclusions in this final version. Finally, special thanks must go to my series editor Bernard K. Johnpoll for his support and to the staff of Greenwood Press for their expertise. Needless to say, any errors herein are solely my own.

Judith A. Sabrosky
West Point, N.Y.

From
Rationality
to Liberation

Feminist Thought as Ideology

FEMINISM. THIS WORD MEANS many things to many people. For some, feminism is equated with the Equal Rights Amendment, or perhaps, *Ms.* magazine. Feminism might also bring to mind the suffragists, such as Elizabeth Cady Stanton and Susan B. Anthony. For the more practically oriented, feminism is identified with the goals of equality, such as equal pay for equal work, equal employment opportunity, and equal representation in government. Feminism, however, is seldom identified with a body of thought or logically consistent set of beliefs or values. It is not considered to be a set of ideas that provides a framework for the existence of the movements, actions, and claims that predominate in feminist circles today.

There are several reasons why feminism is not thought of as an intellectual tradition. The feminists of the contemporary women's movement are too preoccupied with goal achievement to analyze the tradition that gave them birth. Scholars in the social sciences tend to focus on empirical and behavioral analyses of woman's status, how it has or has not changed over the years, and on attitudinal shifts at a rather superficial level. Those disciplines within the social sciences that should analyze feminism as an intellectual tradition (primarily political theory and intellectual history) have not studied feminist thought as a concise theory or consistent set of ideas. Today a worldwide feminist movement is acknowledged by such developments as the United Nations' International Women's Year. But because the intellectual and philosophical origins of this movement have not been studied as a body of thought, it seems to be a movement without a raison d'être and without consistent direction. The theoretical underpinnings and development of feminism are little known and even less understood. This void in knowledge about feminism is needless. Feminist ideas are well founded in Western thought and history. In fact, feminist thought can be considered an "ideology," an ideology which originated in the eighteenth-century intellectual tradition known as the Enlightenment and which evolved over a period of almost two hundred years.

During the Enlightenment, a new secularism arose as the Roman Church's influence continuously declined in literature, life-styles, art, and science. The root of this shift away from the predominance of God and Church was a new concept of the nature of man. No longer was man conceived of as an evil, fallen being whose only salvation lay with the second coming of the Messiah. Rather, Enlightenment thought considered each man to be his own potential messiah. Man possessed the ability to save himself, if not in heaven then at least on earth. The eyes of man began to focus predominantly on the world around him.

The aftermath of man's new self-image was a reevaluation of man's relationships to nature and society, a focusing on things and events external to man. Enlightenment man became preoccupied with analyzing the facts and events around him rather than with blinding religious dogma. The laws of nature and of nature's God merged. Every part of God's handiwork could be demonstrated reasonably. In Enlightenment analyses of society and nature, reason replaced faith. Fact replaced miraculous visions. Most importantly, the reason and rationality of the Enlightenment *philosophes* led to a belief in the perfectibility of the human race on earth.

These Enlightenment ideals of reason, rationality, and human perfectibility and the consequent questioning of existing society that they engendered inevitably led to an evaluation of the status of woman, as well as man, as a human being to be perfected individually and as a member of society. This is not to conclude that the analysis of woman was unique to the Enlightenment or that this analysis developed solely from Enlightenment thought. In *The Republic* Plato argued that qualified women should be guardians or even philosopher-kings on an equal basis with men. In Book I Chapter 9 of the *Politics*, Aristotle argued that too much independence for women contributed to the downfall of Sparta. What was unique to the Enlightenment were the analyses of women in treatise form written by women.

Without the shackles imposed by the preponderance of medieval religion, a few exceptional women acquired the experience and intellectual development needed to question their own existence. Was woman perfectible? Equally so with man? What roles could and should she assume in society? Was woman rational and reasonable or merely a creature of emotion? These were the questions arising from Enlightenment thought that laid the bases for a feminist ideology—a woman's ideology created by woman, analyzing her own character (or perfectibility) and place in society.

Feminist ideology, thus, possesses a history of almost two hundred years, a history founded on the Enlightenment precepts that created and underlie the contemporary Western world. Feminist ideology of the Enlightenment period, like Enlightenment thought, however, has not been adopted intact by contemporary theorists. The feminist thought of Mary Wollstonecraft, for example, fell far short of later ideologies in contextual scope and analytical sophistication. The first expression of feminist ideology was neither its final nor most complete expression.

It must be borne in mind, however, that feminist ideology is and always has been separate and distinct from feminism as a movement. Few of the renowned feminist activists throughout history were also ideologists. The feminist ideologists, or those women who developed a feminist ideology and consequently laid the framework for activism, were primarily theoreticians and philosophers. They were not concerned with activism themselves, although some of them believed it necessary to alter woman's status in society. Many of them are virtually unknown today, not only to activists within the contemporary women's movement but also to students of history and ideology. Yet, while some of these feminists may be unknown to the contemporary world, they were known to each other. Each ideologist possessed knowledge of the writings of at least one of her ideological predecessors. Feminist ideology is therefore a consistent body of thought that evolved over time. Feminist thought became ideology as it was continuously expanded upon and refined. Political theorists and philosophers might object to including feminism with such ideologies as Marxism, liberalism, and democracy. But feminist thought is best understood as ideology. Before discussing feminist thought as ideology, however, it is first necessary to define what is meant by "ideology."

THE NATURE OF IDEOLOGY

Definitions and conceptualizations of "ideology" constructed by philosophers and social scientists during the past two hundred years are almost as numerous as the individuals who constructed them. This wealth of definitions appears to be due to each theorist developing a conception of ideology to fit the requirements of his own inquiry, intellectual background, and/or *Weltanschauung.* Ideology thus not only possesses different meanings for different people, but also performs different functions. In some usages, "ideology" carries pejorative connotations. The label "ideological" implies subjectivity, utopianism, and the imposition of values. Contrarily, "ideology" functions as a neutral methodological tool providing guidelines and a framework for analyzing and evaluating types of political thinking that fall within its scope.

Since the concept "ideology" will be used to analyze the evolution of feminist ideology, an acceptable definition of it must either be found in the history of the term or be constructed. History provides many definitions. Yet none seem appropriate for the study of feminist thought. The first documented usage of the term "ideology" occurred within a few years after the first treatise on women was published in 1792. The individual credited with developing the term was the Frenchman Destutt de Tracy, who later was classified as an "Ideologue" along with other French intellectuals of his school of thought. For de Tracy, "ideology" was a philosophical term describing any "general doctrine about ideas." Ideology was not a name for a particular doctrine or set of ideas, such as the thought of John Locke. Nor did it refer to a particular type of doctrine, for example, a prescriptive or utopian body of ideas. Ideology was instead a neutral term for analyzing the deductive construction of a system or doctrine or ideas.

> It is possible to call this science ideology, paying attention to its subject—general grammar, considering it as a medium—and Logic, considering its purpose. Whatever name it's given, it necessarily includes these three aspects. Ideology seems to me a general term, because the science of ideas is that of expression and deduction.[1]

Both the popularization and disparagement of the term "ideology" were accomplished by Napoleon and Chateaubriand. Napoleon concluded that the French Ideologues were his enemies because they utilized the new science of ideology to justify the destruction of traditional beliefs and structures. He initiated a campaign against the science of *idéologie*. For the first time since its inception, "ideology" assumed negative connotations. It was revolutionary, utopian, and hence a dangerous mode of thought.

Later use of the term "ideology" by Marx and Engels, particularly in *The German Ideology*, perpetuated its negative connotations. For Marx, ideology was "the refusal to recognize this, the real relationship between material existence and ideas."[2] In other words, "an ideology is a more or less systematically developed and explicitly integrated group of ideas [idea taken in the Marxian sense of idea], the subject matter of which belongs to theology, metaphysics, ethics, politics, or jurisprudence."[3] Since for Marx theology, metaphysics, ethics, politics, and jurisprudence all were responsible for the alienation of men because they served class interests and reinforced the dysfunctional social, political, and economic systems, ideology as a composite of these mistaken sets of ideas should be criticized and eventually eliminated.

In the twentieth century, Karl Mannheim in *Ideology and Utopia* introduced the discussion of ideology to social science. Mannheim sought a compromise between the early neutral conception of ideology and Marx's pejorative use of the term. A major contribution to the definition of ideology was Mannheim's distinction between two types, both of which he felt were value-laden. "Ideologies" were the interest and value-bound interpretations of the social, economic, and political spheres made by ruling classes in order to justify and preserve the status quo. "Utopias" were the interest-bound evaluations of existing society made by the oppressed, or those opposed to the status quo, who looked forward to a future in which their needs would be met. In his definition of ideology, then, Mannheim identified essentially the same concept that Marx had implied: ideas that justify the status quo. Yet, in his definition of Utopia, Mannheim deviated from Marx. For Mannheim, Marx's communism could be classified as utopian, first, because Marx failed to identify his own biases, and second, because Marx was simplistic in assuming that class position determined ideology.

Mannheim's most important contribution to the analysis of ideology, however, was his concern with eliminating distortion from ideological construction. Mannheim contended that ideologies, or any formulations evolving from political inquiry, did not evolve in a vacuum. Each ideology is distorted by the *Weltanschauung* (or perspective) that the inquirer brings to his analysis. In other words, ideologies as ideas and bodies of thought are molded by the values, beliefs, and world view of their creator. Ideology could become less distorted and more value-free, however, if the political inquirer or ideologist were aware of his perspective and compensated for it when formulating his ideology. Mannheim unfortunately failed to specify how a person counteracts his own *Weltanschauung*.

Since Mannheim published *Ideology and Utopia*, and particularly in the post-World War II period, controversy over the nature and scope of ideology has become a continuous subject of analysis within the social sciences. Some theorists in the 1950s, most notably Daniel Bell, proclaimed that ideology was dead. Other theorists vigorously refuted Bell's assertion. The result of this controversy has been a continuous dialogue on ideology which has produced many new definitions of ideology, both value-laden and neutral in nature and both applying to particular modes of thought or methodological tools. These diverse definitions have served only to further confuse the meaning of "ideology."

In *The Web of Government*, for example, Robert MacIver defined ideology as "any scheme of thinking characteristic of a group or class."[4] T.W. Adorno et al. asserted in *The Authoritarian Personality*, "The term ideology stand[s] for an organization of opinions, attitudes, and values—a way of thinking about man and society . . . those which exist at a particular time are results of both historical processes and of contemporary social events."[5]

David E. Apter in *The Politics of Modernization* conceived of ideology as

> a generic term applying to general ideas that are potent in specific situations of conduct. For example, not *any* ideals, but political ones; not *any* values, but those establishing a given set of preferences; not *any* beliefs, but those governing particular modes of thought. Because it is the link between action and fundamental belief, ideology helps make more explicit the moral basis of action.[6]

Contemporary definitions and conceptions of ideology may be classified by their content as well as discussed in chronological order. Some definitions are neutral and focus on static terms, such as class or group. An example of the latter is Maurice Parmalee's definition in the *Dictionary of Sociology.* "Ideology. The aggregate of the ideas, beliefs, and modes of thinking characteristic of a group, such as a nation, class, caste, profession or occupation, religious sect, political party, etc."[7]

Other neutral definitions of ideology focus on dynamic factors, that is, on patterns of ideas or beliefs that give general and specific directives of political and/or social action. While some definitions may appear to be value-laden, they are really value-free but stress a value orientation. In other words, they define "ideology" in much the same way that Mannheim defined utopia. J.S. Roucek in "A History of the Concept of Ideology," for instance, defined ideology as

> strictly a system of ideas elaborated in the light of certain conceptions of what "ought to be." It designates a theory of social life which approaches facts from the point of view of an ideal, and interprets them, consciously or unconsciously, to prove the correctness of its analysis and to justify that ideal.[8]

Carl J. Friedrich conceived of an ideology as "syndromes of action-oriented ideas . . . [that] typically contain a program and a strategy for its realization, its operational code."[9]

Among more recent definitions of ideology, the following incorporate, at least minimally, most of the components of ideology identified in the previous definitions, for example, groups, values, and actions. In *Ideology and Participation,* Douglas E. Ashford defined ideology as "the interaction of ideas and behavior around a shared set of political values."[10] William T. Bluhm in *Ideologies and Attitudes,* quoting from Robert M. MacIver, gives a longer but similar definition:

> A political and social ideology . . . is a system of political, economic, and social values and ideas from which objectives are derived. These objectives form the nucleus of a political program. . . . Often they

form a complete, harmonious, and consistent system of explanation of the purpose of society and of the surrounding social, economic, and political phenomena. Setting forth dynamic and practical objectives to influence future social and political developments, they try—with a most ambitious design—to decide mankind's destiny.[11]

Despite the diversity of these definitions of ideology, none is suited for an analysis of feminist thought as ideology. Each of these definitions lacks some component included in another definition. Because feminist thought has not been studied as ideology previously, the most stringent definition of the term possible is required. Otherwise, it could be asserted that if a more comprehensive definition of ideology were used, feminism would not qualify as ideology. Therefore, for the purposes of this study, a definition or conception of ideology was developed that incorporates *all* the components of ideology mentioned in the previously given definitions. If feminist thought satisfies this definition of ideology, then it should satisfy any other definition.

A comprehensive definition of ideology may be constructed by combining the ideas of two theorists who sought a standardization of the term "ideology" for use in political inquiry. They hoped to provide a basis for uniformly analyzing ideologies and making them "responsible." In defining ideology, both drew upon most of the definitions previously mentioned in conceptualizing the scope, content, and application of ideology to political inquiry. The two theorists are William E. Connolly, author of *Political Science and Ideology,* who was heavily indebted to Karl Mannheim, and Willard A. Mullins, author of "On the Concept of Ideology in Political Science," who to a lesser extent was indebted to Karl Marx.

Connolly's simplistic definition of ideology incorporates the major components of most accepted definitions of ideology. He concluded that

an ideology is an integrated set of beliefs about the social and political environment. It purports to tell us how the system is organized, which desired goals can be promoted, what agencies and channels can most effectively be employed to forward the goals in the given setting, and what the required action will cost various groups in the short and long run in terms of status, power, happiness, wealth, and so on.[12]

In other words, Connolly defined ideology as (1) a set of beliefs and hypotheses (about the system and desired goals); (2) recommendations for action in terms of the means (including specific actors) to achieve specified ends; and (3) the intended consequences of any actions taken to implement goals. If any body of thought were to classify as an "ideology" according to Connolly's definition, it should include analyses of the system as it exists, the desired system that incorporates delineated goals and objectives, and recommendations for ways to implement these goals and objectives. However, because of its descriptive nature, Connolly's definition poses problems for the theorist. While it certainly discusses what the components of an ideology should be, it ignores any analysis of how an ideology functions, what it does, or how to evaluate whether it is good or bad.

Mullins's endeavor to conceptualize ideology, while lacking because it does not describe the content of ideology, fills the void in Connolly's analysis. He developed a functional definition of ideology, defining ideology

> as a logically coherent system of symbols which, within a more or less sophisticated conception of history, links the cognitive and evaluative perception of one's social condition—especially its prospects for the future—to a program of collective action for the maintenance, alteration or transformation of society.[13]

Thus for Mullins, ideology consists of five interrelated functional characteristics. First, ideology incorporates a modern conception of historical consciousness. That is, historical consciousness operates within ideology to discriminate between the past, present, and future and to define the goals and objectives that Connolly concluded are parts of the composite called ideology. Historical change replaces tradition as a sufficient guide to human action and shaping the future.

The second functional component of ideology in Mullins's definition is ideology's cognitive power. The cognitive power or function of ideology consists of its inherent normative values and opinions. These normative values function to justify desires for change by appealing to human wants and aspirations. The adoption and promotion of Connolly's desired goals, therefore, are dependent upon the degree of cognitive power in an ideology. If the ideology in moral or normative terms does not justify the creation of new goals and substantiate them in moral terms, then the new goals probably will not be supported or promoted.

Except for historical consciousness, the evaluative power of an ideology is the most important functional component of Mullins's analysis. An ideology must evaluate not only the existing social and political arrangements but also what is conceived for the future. In evaluating the existing environment, an ideology determines which aspects of this environment inhibit achievement of the desired goals. Only after such an analysis can effective actions be developed to change the environment and implement the ideology's goals. The ideology similarly must evaluate the future in order to determine if the actions defined are capable of achieving the desired ends. The evaluative power of ideology thus functions in all three of Connolly's components of ideology—the analysis of system organization, recommendations for action, and the intended consequences—by analyzing the costs and benefits of any actions.

Ideology's action orientation in Mullins's definition is the characteristic that is most similar to Connolly's descriptive definition. Connolly concluded that an ideology must delineate the intended consequences of goal achievement. In other words, action must be defined not only in terms of "what must be done" but also in terms of "what will be achieved." The consequences of action should be consistent with the ideology's desired goals, both in terms of who benefits and who suffers from the ideology's implementation. For example, if an ideology's goal is economic equality in a society of severe economic differentiation among classes, and if one economically deprived class elevates its economic position at the expense of an equally deprived class, then the consequences of action are inconsistent with the desired goals and normative position of the ideology.

Mullins's functional action orientation is similar. "The significance of ideology in mobilization is not that it 'causes one to do' but that it 'gives one cause for doing.' It provides grounds or warrants for the political activity engaged in."[14] In other words, Mullins believed that in an ideology action should be consistent with ideals and values. The valuations and goals of an ideology justify action.

If the action is inconsistent with the normative prescriptions of the ideology, then it cannot be justified.

The final functional characteristic of ideology that Mullins defined is not incorporated in Connolly's definition. Mullins contended that an ideology must have "logical coherence" or must "make sense." Ideology "facilitates a logical grasp of events and situations . . . can be written down and its truths 'worked out' . . . tends to explicate the significance of events, situations and possible courses of human actions."[15] By an ideology that progresses logically, Mullins meant that goals follow from an evaluation of the system and that actions are derived from goals.

From these two conceptions of ideology, a composite definition of ideology is easily constructed. "Ideology" may be defined as a body of thought that incorporates the following elements: (1) a set of beliefs about how the political, social, and economic environments operate that is constructed from analyses and evaluations made of the societal system; (2) a set of desired goals that purport to change the existing system in some way. These goals are derived from the application of normative and moral values to existing society and define, given the historical context—or *Weltanschauung*—of the society, which changes should take place to make society more consistent with the values delineated; and (3) a program of action that would best implement the goals—best in terms of being feasible (having the best chance of being successful) and best in terms of this means being consistent with the desired ends, that is, consistent with the ideology and normative values that initiated desires for change.

FEMINIST THOUGHT AS IDEOLOGY

This definition of ideology attempts to integrate the two traditional approaches to conceptualizing ideology. The definition is constructed as a neutral methodological tool for evaluating feminist ideology or, for that matter, any ideology. But it also takes into consideration, and hopefully provides a mechanism for compensating for, the value preferences and *Weltanschauungen* of feminist ideologists. To satisfy this definition of ideology, any body of thought must be comprehensive, not merely a polemical treatise mistakenly identified as ideology.

When applying this definition of ideology to feminist thought, the following specific ideas are analyzed. Part One of the definition, the set of beliefs about how the societal system operates, is used to identify how feminist ideologists have viewed their and other women's relationship to society, their power or lack of power within or over societal institutions, their societal roles, permitted occupations, educational opportunities, rights in marriage, law, and politics, and so on. The analysis, in other words, focuses on how the political and social environments operate for women, what the environments both permit and forbid women to do. Part Two of the definition, the statement of goals that purport to change the system, when applied to feminist ideology permits analysis and evaluation of recommended prescriptions for women's future roles within society. Both how society and women's roles within society generally and in the areas mentioned in Part One should be changed are identified. Part Three, the definition of a program of action to achieve the prescriptions, leads to delineation of both short- and long-term programs and strategies to implement feminist prescriptions and long-range goals.

While this approach to classifying and evaluating feminist thought as ideology is a feasible endeavor, its application is not as clear-cut or as simple as with other ideologies. Feminist ideology, as we shall see, differs significantly from other ideologies in two respects. These differences have a significant impact upon its analysis. First, unlike ideologies such as Marxism or liberalism, feminist ideology lacks one or even a small group of prominent proponents. Feminism is and always has been a composite of ideas and writings of a diverse group of women—diverse geographically, in intellectual traditions, in time, and hence in *Weltanschauungen.* Second, feminism as an ideology evolved slowly and incrementally over a period of almost two hundred years. Initially, feminists were more concerned with criticizing their states in society than with prescribing goals for the future. Later, feminists of the mid- and late-nineteenth century were almost utopian in their emphases on futuristic goals. Yet others, particularly twentieth-century feminists, focused almost exclusively on action or how to achieve the defined goals.

These differences, when considered together, render the study of feminist ideology difficult. Unlike communism, for example, which developed at the height of the industrial revolution, feminism's evolution proceeded through a variety of social and economic environments. With each new socioeconomic environment (from the industrial revolution almost to the post-industrial state), feminist ideology correspondingly changed in reaction to its new environment.

Given feminism's evolution over a long period of time, another important influence on the development of feminism as an ideology must be evaluated. As socioeconomic environments changed over time, so did intellectual environments. In identifying the important feminist thinkers, we find that they came from diverse intellectual heritages spanning two continents. In order to understand the complete impact that the changing environments and *Weltanschauungen* exerted on feminist ideology, we must also analyze the relationship of each feminist ideologist to her intellectual world—to which intellectual traditions she was indebted and to what extent.

This exercise will attempt to make feminist ideology "responsible." According to Connolly,

> *The fully responsible ideology is one in which there is a serious and continuing effort to formulate publicly all of the factors that influence decisions at each stage of inquiry.* In a responsible ideology there is a serious effort to clarify for self and others the organization of the *perspective* brought to inquiry; there is a publicly developed *interpretation* of relevant events and trends at a level of abstraction high enough to cover the problem area; there is a publicly stated *moral and political stand*, in which specific actions are suggested to resolve (or adjust to) the identified problem.[16]

While an ideology's creator usually takes into account his own *Weltanschauung* at the time of creation, it is necessary to make feminism responsible ex post facto. As we shall see, feminist ideology is so heavily indebted to the *Weltanschauungen* of its creators that its sources, development, and validity cannot be determined without an understanding of the environments within which it developed. Thus, the privately held belief systems of the predominant feminist ideologists must be made public, to the extent that that is possible in retrospect, in order to provide a framework within which future critics and analysts of feminist ideology may work.

In delineating the perspectives (or intellectual heritages) of feminist ideologists, the following factors must be considered. First, the systems of beliefs and values held by the ideologists that provided the framework for their evaluations of women's existing status in society and influenced the development of desired goals must be identified. The sources of these values and beliefs may be found in the feminists's intellectual writings, education, and personal associations. Second, how these existing values and beliefs were incorporated in feminist ideology and how dependent present-day feminist ideology is on the value and belief systems of other ideologies should be determined. And third, as the ultimate purpose of this exercise, the uniqueness of feminist ideology should be evaluated.

In summary, this endeavor is an attempt to prove that feminist thought is an ideology that can be classified, analyzed, and evaluated according to a rigid definition of ideology. The strengths and weaknesses of feminist ideology as a set of beliefs about the nature of society, prescriptions and goals for changing society, and the means for implementing change are evaluated. This analysis and evaluation of feminist thought as ideology, though, proceeds on several assumptions. Since no standard and widely accepted definition of ideology exists within the social sciences, it was necessary to construct a definition of ideology. The comprehensiveness of this definition may be troublesome to some because it eliminates some well-known contemporary feminist treatises as ideology and contests their importance to the development of feminist thought.

A second assumption is that any body of thought may be classified as ideology despite the nature of its source as long as it satisfies the requirements of an acceptable definition of ideology. Since feminist ideology is composed of the thought of many ideologists and lacks one or even a few major proponents, no single work may be identified as representative of feminist ideology. This diversity of feminist ideology means that it must be studied chronologically rather than as a single complete body of thought.

The third assumption is that feminist ideology did not evolve along a continuum from initial analyses of woman's status in society to an ideology. Because of the diverse *Weltanschauungen* of its proponents, feminist ideology suffered several regressions in development. Objective analyses of prescriptions for woman's status in society were briefly replaced in feminist thought by the goals of other ideologies and movements. This occurred particularly in the nineteenth century during the Abolitionist and socialist movements. Thus, in analyzing the development of feminist ideology, some renowned works that theoretically could be classified as ideology are only briefly mentioned because they contributed nothing to the development of feminist thought as an ideology.

Finally, choosing works to be analyzed as feminist ideology also posed problems. Hundreds of feminist works have been published in the past two hundred years. The problem is that most of them were either polemical or utopian, or had shaky philosophical bases. To eliminate these types of works from consideration, only feminist treatises that incorporated at least two elements of the definition of ideology were selected. Also, as was previously mentioned, all of the thinkers chosen for analysis built their ideologies upon the thought of earlier feminist thinkers. This requirement was necessary to prove that feminist ideology is a tradition and that it evolved as a consistent and interrelated set of ideas.

While some assumptions must be made if feminist thought is to be analyzed as ideology, they do not warrant abandoning its study. The content of feminist thought more than justifies treating it as ideology. In other words, feminist ideology may not be expounded in one or two comprehensive treatises, but its content as it developed over two hundred years fulfills all the requirements of both descriptive and functional definitions of ideology. As a body of thought and set of ideas, feminism today is an ideology. The goals and programs of feminist ideology, although not always known by contemporary feminist activists or by social scientists, initiated the development of the feminist movement that exists today by inciting feminist activism in the nineteenth century, which in turn served as a precedent for modern feminist movements. Because of both its ideological content and its importance for understanding the contemporary feminist movement, feminist ideology should be studied.

To facilitate this study, feminist thinkers are evaluated herein as ideologists by being discussed as representatives of specific ideological traditions. Mary Wollstonecraft was a member of the Enlightenment tradition. Flora Tristan and Frances Wright were utopian socialists. Sarah Grimké was an Abolitionist. Margaret Fuller and Elizabeth Oakes Smith were part of the Transcendentalist circle led by Ralph Waldo Emerson. And Simone de Beauvoir followed the existentialist philosophy of Jean-Paul Sartre. Although these feminists were the primary contributors to feminist ideology, other feminist thinkers representing other ideological perspectives are discussed as well for their less comprehensive, but still significant, impacts upon feminist ideology's evolution.

The contributions each thinker made to the development of feminist ideology and her indebtedness to her ideological perspective are analyzed together. In each case, contributions to feminist ideology were derived from a broader ideology. The objective of this study, therefore, is simple. It seeks to demonstrate that feminist thought, first of all, is an ideology and, second, is constructed from the values, methodologies, and programs for change of other ideologies. Consequently, this study also includes determinations of which ideological traditions the different components of feminist ideology were derived from.

This analysis begins in Chapter 2 with a discussion of the precursors of feminist ideology—Mary Wollstonecraft and the utopian socialist feminists—who laid the foundations of feminist thought. Chapter 3 continues the investigation with an analysis of Sarah Grimké and Margaret Fuller. These two feminist thinkers constructed the first true variants of feminist ideology. Chapter 4 evaluates the "middle years" of feminist ideology, with particular emphasis on the impact of the women's suffrage movement and the Nineteenth Amendment on feminist ideology. In Chapter 5 there is a discussion of contemporary feminism which leads to the identification of the "theoretician" of contemporary feminism. And last, Chapter 6 evaluates the strengths and weaknesses of feminist ideology as it exists today and also makes recommendations for future directions in the development of feminist ideology.

NOTES

1. Destutt de Tracy, quoted in Arne Naess, *Democracy, Ideology and Objectivity—Studies in the Semantics and Cognitive Analysis of Ideological Controversy* (Oxford: Basil Blackwell, 1956), p. 149.

2. Karl Marx, quoted in Judith N. Shklar, ed., *Political Theory and Ideology* (New York: The Macmillan Company, 1966), p.5.

3. Naess, *Democracy*, p. 160.

4. Robert M. MacIver, *The Web of Government*, quoted in Naess, *Democracy*, p. 162.

5. T.W. Adorno, *The Authoritarian Personality*, quoted in Robert E. Lane, "The Meanings of Ideology," in *Power, Participation and Ideology*, ed. Calvin J. Larson and Philo C. Washburn (New York: David McKay, 1969), p. 322.

6. David E. Apter, *The Politics of Modernization* (Chicago: University of Chicago Press, 1965), p. 314.

7. Maurice Parmalee, *Dictionary of Sociology*, quoted in Naess, *Democracy*, p. 162.

8. J. S. Roucek, "A History of the Concept of Ideology," *Journal of the History of Ideas* 5(October 1944):279.

9. Carl J. Friedrich, "Ideology in Politics: A Theoretical Comment," *Slavic Review* 24(1965):612.

10. Douglas E. Ashford, *Ideology and Participation*, Sage Library of Social Research, vol. 3 (Beverly Hills, Ca.: Sage, 1972), p. 13.

11. Robert M. MacIver, quoted in William T. Bluhm, *Ideologies and Attitudes: Modern Political Culture* (Englewood Cliffs, N.J.: Prentice-Hall, Inc., 1974), p. 3.

12. William E. Connolly, *Political Science and Ideology* (New York: Atherton Press, 1967), p. 2.

13. Willard A. Mullins, "On the Concept of Ideology in Political Science," *American Political Science Review* 66 (June 1972):510.

14. Ibid., p. 509.

15. Ibid., p. 506.

16. Connolly, *Ideology*, p. 137.

The Precursors of Feminist Ideology

Chapter Two

FEMINIST IDEOLOGY ORIGINATED WITHIN the two intellectual traditions that marked the beginning of the modern world—the Enlightenment and utopian socialism. While neither tradition was specifically concerned with the status of woman, both ideologies sought to improve the quality of life for man in general. They reflected a belief that man was innately perfectible and that he could become a rational, thinking being. Both envisioned radical societal change as the method for improving the status of all men.

Three women who were members of these traditions recognized the applicability of their values and goals to woman's place in the world. Consciously utilizing the values and analyses of their ideological perspectives, they hypothesized about what woman might become if the prescriptions recommended for each ideology were applied to woman. None of the women developed her analysis of woman sufficiently to construct a comprehensive ideology. But all three contributed significantly to the future development of a feminist ideology by setting precedents and laying the groundwork for future feminist ideologists. Thus, as the Enlightenment *philosophes* and utopian socialists laid the bases for Marxism and liberalism, so these three feminists were the precursors of feminist ideology. Although their analyses were simplistic by present-day standards, their impact on later feminists led to the development of a feminist ideology. Their importance lies both in this fact and in their role as the first women to make a conscious attempt to criticize woman's status in society and to envision and advocate a more equal place.

Mary Wollstonecraft was the Enlightenment figure who desired to "enlighten" woman in addition to man. The Frenchwoman Flora

Tristan and the American Frances Wright were the utopian socialists who applied the socialist vision to woman.

MARY WOLLSTONECRAFT: THE BEGINNING

Mary Wollstonecraft was an Enlightenment woman, as her three most important treatises reveal. The *Rights of Men* was a clear exposition of the Enlightenment belief in reason and in the inherent perfectibility of man. *An Historical and Moral View of the Origin and Progress of the French Revolution and the Effect It Has Produced in Europe* underlined her Enlightenment beliefs in understanding and reason. And her *A Vindication of the Rights of Woman* expressed Wollstonecraft's feminist thoughts.

Wollstonecraft spent her life within a circle of prominent Enlightenment theorists. William Godwin in his *Memoirs of Mary Wollstonecraft* emphasized the breadth of Wollstonecraft's, his wife's, personal associations. "It is almost unnecessary to mention, that she was personally acquainted with the majority of leaders of the French Revolution."[1] Allene Gregory in *The French Revolution and the English Novel* observed, "Paine, Horne, Cooke, Fordyce, Godwin, Fuseli, Holcroft, and all their brilliant circle welcome her as an equal."[2] Janet M. Todd in her Introduction to Wollstonecraft's *French Revolution* concluded that Wollstonecraft was a member of a circle of radical thinkers which served as a forum for her rationalism and provided her with a "structure and language for her arguments."[3] In addition to being accepted as a member by the intellectual circle of Enlightenment figures of the late eighteenth century, the public respected Wollstonecraft's contributions to Enlightenment thought.[4]

But what distinguished Mary Wollstonecraft from other representatives of the Enlightenment was her contribution to feminist ideology. Shortly after her death, her husband William Godwin wrote the following evaluation of her *A Vindication of the Rights of Woman:*

The Vindication of the Rights of Woman is undoubtedly a very unequal performance, and eminently deficient in method and arrangement. When tried by the hoary and long-established laws of literary composition, it can scarcely maintain its claim to be placed in the first class of human productions. But when we consider the importance of its doctrines, and the eminence of genius it displays, it seems not very improbable that it will be read as long as the English language endures. The publication of the book forms an epocha in the subject to which it belongs; and Mary Wollstonecraft will per-haps here-after be found to have performed more substantial service for the cause of her sex, than all the other writers, male or female, that ever felt themselves animated in the behalf of oppressed and injured beauty.[5]

Today, among contemporary feminists and literary and political critics, this evaluation holds true. The *Vindication* is considered the first significant treatise on women by a woman in Western literature and the first attempt, albeit at times a badly written one, at developing a feminist ideology.

In the *Vindication* Wollstonecraft attempted to analyze the status of woman in the most intellectually sophisticated and democratic societies of her time—Great Britain and France. Her analysis took a comparative approach, focusing on woman's intellectual, social, and political statures relative to those of men. From her evaluation of woman's status, she delineated a set of prescriptions, stating her evaluation of woman's potential in a society in which woman was afforded identical advantages with men, and prescribed a limited course of action for women to take if they wished to acquire equal status.

To the reader of the *Vindication,* Wollstonecraft's evaluations of woman's stature, prescriptions for further development, and pro-gram for achieving change seem very narrow. Because she was concerned primarily with the intellectual and moral equality of woman, political, legal, and economic equality were mentioned only peripherally. Her narrow focus, however, is understandable in light of her life and heritage. She was part of the Enlighten-ment tradition and an intellectual circle that emphasized the im-portance of rationality and rational development for the individual. She devoted herself to intellectual pursuit in an attempt to support her brothers and sisters.

For her time, however, Wollstonecraft's claims for intellectual and moral equality for woman were in themselves extremely radical.

In Great Britain and France in the late eighteenth century, women were seldom educated beyond basic reading, writing, and religious and household knowledge. Even classical education, that is, Latin, Greek, and fundamental mathematics, was considered "indelicate" for a woman and perhaps even beyond her capabilities. Wollstonecraft's assumption that woman could achieve intellectual and moral equality with man contradicted the most famous educators and educational theorists of her time, not the least of whom was Jean-Jacques Rousseau.

The obvious starting point in an analysis of Wollstonecraft's feminist thought is the issue of whether woman is inherently inferior to man. Wollstonecraft asserted that "it cannot be demonstrated that woman is essentially inferior to man because she has always been subjugated,"[6] a statement consistent with her intellectual heritage. Because woman is subjugated, she is unable to develop her reason and rationality. Without the ability to reason, woman cannot determine whether she is innately inferior to man. Wollstonecraft argued, however, that the issue of woman's innate inferiority was ultimately unimportant since woman's inferiority was contrived by man.

> Exalted by their inferiority, they constantly demand homage as women, though experience should teach them that the men who pride themselves upon paying this arbitrary insolent respect to the sex, with the most scrupulous exactness, are most inclined to tyrannize over, and despise, the very weakness they cherish.[7]

Wollstonecraft was most concerned in the *Vindication* with the consequences of woman's inferiority—an inferiority she believed was at least magnified by woman's subjection to man. Subjection and inferiority deleteriously affected woman's character. Because of their subjection, Wollstonecraft viewed women as creatures of pleasure. "Women seek for pleasure as the main purpose of existence."[8] Their common goal of pleasing men allowed for no diversity of female character. "All women are to be levelled, by meekness and docility, into one character of yielding softness and gentle compliance."[9]

In other words, woman's primary concern was to be a woman, a goal and desire that for Wollstonecraft degraded the sex and precluded any intellectual or moral development.

> Women, commonly called Ladies, are not to be contradicted in company, are not allowed any manual strength; and from them the negative virtues only are expected. . . . Besides, by living more with each other, and being seldom absolutely alone, they are more under the influence of sentiments than passions. Solitude and reflection are necessary to give wishes the force of passions . . . and to enable the imagination to enlarge the object, and make it the most desirable.[10]

Woman as Wollstonecraft perceived her in late-eighteenth-century society was thus a creature of pleasure whose sole ambition was to be what she was. Her goals in life were to attract men and maintain a good reputation. The major consequence of these goals was woman's lack of virtue.

The objects of Wollstonecraft's analysis of woman's character, however, were narrower than necessary. "Ladies" were not the only character type that existed in eighteenth-century England and France. Wollstonecraft certainly must have encountered the existence of prostitutes in the cities she inhabited. She could have argued that they also lacked virtue and sought to please men, although concern for their reputations might not have been a moving force in their lives. Additionally, many women in Wollstonecraft's era were forced to earn their own existence (as she herself did) or supplement their husbands' incomes. By the late eighteenth century, particularly in England, women were already working in the textile mills, and rural wives had always contributed their labor to the well-being of the family. These women obviously were not included in Wollstonecraft's analysis.

On whom, then, did Wollstonecraft base her analysis? The most likely answer is the middle class, of which she was a part. The intellectual and social circles in which Wollstonecraft travelled were middle-class groups, the Radical Reformers in particular. The men were primarily civil servants by profession and political and intellectual radicals by avocation. Wollstonecraft exhibited this middle-class identification in several dimensions of her analysis. Her antagonism toward the wealthy and hereditary wealth reflected a middle-class bias. For example, Wollstonecraft discussed the deleterious effects that inherited property had on character development.

> Hereditary property sophisticates the mind, and the unfortunate victims to it, if I may so express myself, swathed from their birth, seldom exert the locomotive faculty of body and mind; and thus viewing everything through one medium, and that a false one, they are unable to discern in what true merit and happiness consist.[11]

And again she argued, "Destructive, however, as riches and inherited honours are to the human character, women are more debased and cramped, if possible, by them than men."[12]

By process of elimination, Wollstonecraft's analysis had to be of middle-class women, the wives and lovers of her male associates. She ignored the class of working women and exhibited a near hatred for the wealthy. This middle-class bias or focus must be kept in mind when analyzing Wollstonecraft's ideology, especially her prescriptions and programs for change, because they too were focused on the middle class.

The consequences of woman's character, in Wollstonecraft's view, was that woman was unable to fulfill adequately the one role in life allowed to her under male domination—that of mother. Since woman was concerned solely with pleasure and gratifying men, she was equipped neither intellectually nor emotionally for raising children.

> To be a good mother—a woman must have sense, and that independence of mind which few women possess who are taught to depend entirely on their husbands. . . . Unless the understanding of woman be enlarged, and her character rendered more firm, by being allowed to govern her own conduct, she will never have sufficient sense of command of temper to manage her children properly.[13]

Woman's failure in this role particularly concerned Wollstonecraft when she developed prescriptions and programs for change.

Wollstonecraft's strong, although biased, analysis of woman's inferior stature in society included extremely detailed analyses of why woman had inferior status and tolerated her inferiority and what social forces developed and maintained that status and inferiority. Simply put, woman accepted her inferiority because male tyranny maintained her ignorance and inferior status.

Woman's ignorance, in Wollstonecraft's analysis, was a self-perpetuating force. Mothers taught their daughters the art and value of being ignorant. This socialization process had become so ingrained in woman's perception of herself that any alternative was either not perceived or blindly ignored. Wollstonecraft summarized this educative process thus: "Women are told from their infancy, and taught by the example of their mothers, that a little knowledge of human weakness, justly termed cunning, softness of temper, *outward* obedience, and a scrupulous attention to a puerile kind of propriety, will obtain for them the protection of man."[14] This socialization, like all child socialization processes, occurred at so young an age that the individual girl lacked the ability to question or reject what she was being taught.[15] Ignorance was inculcated into women so thoroughly that it became not merely a way of life to be tolerated, but one to be sought. "Considering the length of time that women have been dependent, is it surprising that some of them hug their chains, and fawn like the spaniel?"[16]

It is difficult to imagine that women in Wollstonecraft's era, a period in history of democratic ideologies and revolutions that asserted the rights of men, desired ignorance. Woman remained complacent, according to Wollstonecraft, because lack of education rendered her unable to possess the understanding and reason necessary to question or alter her status. Education negatively affected woman and rendered her unable to perceive or initiate change in her status. "The little knowledge which women of strong minds attain, is, from various circumstances, of a more desultory kind than the knowledge of men."[17] For Wollstonecraft, then, woman's education did not serve an intellectual function. Instead it reinforced the mother-to-daughter socialization process that conceived of woman as a creature of ignorance and pleasure. "In short, the whole tenor of female education (the education of society) tends to render the best disposed romantic and inconstant; and the remainder vain and mean."[18]

Woman completely lacked the power of reason, that is, the power to discern truth. Woman could not reason because "man [was] ever placed between her and reason, [and] she is always represented as only created to see through a gross medium, and to take things on trust."[19] Wollstonecraft did not deny the possibility that the lack of reason could be innate to woman's physical and/or moral nature. But she seemed to believe that the quality of education and the socialization of ignorance *could* in themselves have suffered woman to be unable to reason.

> In tracing the causes that, in my opinion, have degraded woman . . . to me it appears clear that they all spring from want of understanding. Whether this arises from a physical or accidental weakness of faculties, time alone can determine, for I shall not lay any great stress on the example of a few women who, from having received a masculine education, have acquired courage and resolution; I only contend that men who have been placed in similar situations, have acquired a similar character—I speak of bodies of men, and that men of genius and talents have started out of a class, in which women have never yet been placed.[20]

The social forces that developed and maintained woman's inferiority were, secondarily, hereditary riches, the existence of ranks in society, political inequality, and, primarily, male tyranny. Woman might have improved her character through the development of reason and understanding had she been free from the external restraints that confined her. It was these very restraints, however, that denied her the freedom to develop her intellect and question her status.

Hereditary wealth was more destructive of the female than the male character because woman had no freedom to counteract the negative effects of wealth as men did. "Men may still, in some degree, unfold their faculties by becoming soldiers and statesmen."[21] Similarly, distinctions of rank were more crippling for women than men. "There are some loopholes out of which a man may creep, and dare to think and act for himself; but for a woman it is a herculean task, because she has difficulties peculiar to her sex to overcome which require almost superhuman powers."[22] The lack of political privileges also inhibited the development of woman's reason and understanding because it forced her inward upon herself, reinforcing her desires for pleasure and a good reputation. Without political

privileges, woman had few, if any, avenues of activities and opportunities open to her.

> Females, in fact, denied all political privileges, and not allowed, as
> married women, excepting in criminal cases, a civil existence, have
> their attention naturally drawn from the interest of the whole com-
> munity to that of the minute parts, though the private duty of any
> member of society must be very imperfectly performed when not
> connected with the general good.[23]

The cause of these oppressive societal factors was obvious for
Wollstonecraft—male tyranny. The responsibility for woman's
inferiority was unequivocally man's. "I shall only insist that men
have increased that inferiority till women are almost sunk below
the standard of rational creatures."[24] "Men, indeed, appear to me
to act in a very unphilosophical manner when they try to secure the
good conduct of women by attempting to keep them always in a
state of childhood."[25]

Male tyranny was a product of the ages. Man used his initial
dominance, derived from the time when physical strength was the
criterion of power, to structure society to exclude women and keep
them inferior. Governments were constructed to strip women of
their reason. Woman, therefore, was always a slave or despot. Civil
governments created civil and legal structures to further render
woman inferior.[26] Other methods men devised to dominate woman
were polygamy and their emphasis on the value of physical beauty.
For men, Wollstonecraft asserted, "beauty" could be a product of
the mind as well as the body, while for woman, beauty indicated
physical perfection.[27]

In summary, Wollstonecraft's analysis in the *Vindication* of the
status of women in eighteenth-century Britain and France was comprehensive. She defined, as we have seen, the instruments and
effects of male tyranny on the female character and woman's role
in society. Woman, for Wollstonecraft, barely qualified as a human
being because external factors inhibited her ability to reason. This
emphasis on reason and understanding as the criteria for measuring
human development and fulfillment was part of the Enlightenment
tradition.

Wollstonecraft, however, did not limit the *Vindication* to criticisms of woman's status. She developed prescriptions for improving the condition of woman in society and for woman's individual development. Wollstonecraft's ultimate goal was to render woman equal to man in virtue, reason, and independence. Education was her most important prescription for woman's future development.

Education should be equal for men and women not only in content but in its effects on the individual. Knowledge should become equally accessible regardless of sex, since only through knowledge can the individual become virtuous. "To render also the social compact truly equitable, and in order to spread those enlightening principles which alone can meliorate the fate of man, women must be allowed to found their virtue on knowledge, which is scarcely possible unless they be educated by the same pursuits as men."[28] Only through virtue would man, used in the generic sense, be truly enlightened.

Wollstonecraft did not argue, however, that men and women should necessarily acquire the same amount or level of knowledge. The contextual scope of knowledge should be identical, that is, mathematics, the classics, literature, and science should be studied by both men and women to impart knowledge of nature which is part of God. But on the degree of knowledge that woman should attain, Wollstonecraft again reneged on determining or concluding whether woman's inferiority was innate. On two separate occasions when discussing the acquisition of knowledge, Wollstonecraft admitted of the possibility that woman might indeed be so inferior to man that she could not hope to reach his intellectual level.

The *knowledge* of the two sexes should be the same in nature, if not in degree, and . . . women, considered not only as moral, but rational creatures, ought to endeavour to acquire human virtues (or perfections) by the *same* means as men, instead of being educated like a fanciful kind of *half* being—one of Rousseau's wild chimeras.[29]

Further, should experience prove that they cannot attain the same degree of strength of mind, perseverance, and fortitude, let their virtues be the same in kind, though they may vainly struggle for the same degree; and the superiority of man will be equally clear, if not clearer; and truth, as it is a simple principle, which admits of no modification, would be common to both.[30]

Wollstonecraft's primary goal thus seems to have been to provide woman with opportunities for education and then to see what woman did with those opportunities. This general theme arose in several places where Wollstonecraft discussed the possibility of innate female inferiority. She seemed almost preoccupied with testing whether or not woman possessed the capabilities to become man's equal, to the detriment of pressing for any real advantages for woman. Her prescription was to provide woman with a smattering of equality—in other words, with the same scope of intellectual experiences as man. Nowhere in the *Vindication* did Wollstonecraft prescribe equality for woman for equality's sake. Her arguments were not based on a democratic concern for individual self-realization through equal status, especially political status. It appears that instead Wollstonecraft was bound to her Enlightenment rationalist heritage, arguing that woman's inferiority was detrimental to the moral progress of the race because she was unable to educate her children adequately. Female equality to Wollstonecraft was a goal not for woman's sake alone but for the improvement of society as a whole.

Wollstonecraft was concerned, nonetheless, with achieving independence for woman. She even argued that woman should possess enough education to support herself economically if necessary. But again, self-determination and economic independence were endorsed not out of a democratic concern for equality, but rather because work and the responsibility of self-support strengthened the mind. Woman should have self-determination because it developed virtue. "Virtue, like everything valuable, must be loved for herself alone; or she will not take up her abode with us."[31]

Thus, in the *Vindication*, the seemingly democratic ideals of self-determination and independence, freedom of mind and individual development, were instead part of the Enlightenment concern for moral development. Woman's responsibility as a free and self-determining being in Wollstonecraft's analysis was not to her country but to herself as a rational creature. Only secondarily should woman possess the duties of citizenship, the most important of which Wollstonecraft defined as motherhood.[32] "The conclusion that I wish to draw is obvious; make women rational creatures, and free citizens, and they will quickly become good wives and mothers; that is—if men do not neglect the duties of husbands and fathers."[33]

The program that Wollstonecraft developed for implementing her educational prescriptions was very sketchy, especially in her definition of the scope of woman's education. She posited no plan for initiating any system of uniform or comprehensive education for woman, nor was she concerned with who would teach woman as later feminists were. Wollstonecraft merely advocated that girls and boys should play, exercise, and be educated together. If girls played with boys, their rationality might develop further.[34] If girls underwent the same physical exercise as boys, "we may know how far the natural superiority of man extends."[35] Coeducation would enable woman to be a more rational creature, thus making her a better wife, an important consideration for Wollstonecraft.

In the economic and political areas Wollstonecraft half-heartedly recommended strategies that woman might pursue in the distant future, but she offered no concrete guidance. For example, when she discussed equal representation in government, she weakened her statement by concluding, "But, as the whole system of representation is now in this country only a convenient handle for despotism, they need not complain, for they are as well represented as a numerous class of hard-working mechanics."[36] When Wollstonecraft claimed that woman might make a good physician or perform well in politics, she similarly failed to delineate how woman should gain access to these areas.

In conclusion, Wollstonecraft's prescriptions and programs for achieving a certain degree of equality for woman greatly weakened her original analysis of woman's condition in society. Her concern for equality was not that it would benefit woman per se but that equality for woman, primarily in education, would greatly increase the degree of virtue in society and man. Wollstonecraft made no arguments for the innate equality of woman, even in the intellectual sphere. This is understandable, however, considering that Mary Wollstonecraft brought to her analysis of woman an Enlightenment perspective. The vocabulary she employed in her analysis—nature, natural rights, reason, rationality, experience, understanding, rational religion, human perfectibility—was the vocabulary of the Enlightenment. The goals she established for woman were the

Enlightenment's goals for men. The beginnings of a feminist ideology thus may be traced to the Enlightenment *philosophes.*

For the *philosophes,* nature was the standard for determining whether ideas, customs, and the institutions of men were perfect, for a perfect human institution must be in harmony with nature. Natural law for the *philosophes* was the doctrine that man possessed individual rights that were more fundamental than political, economic, and social laws. These natural rights included the right to individual happiness, harmony, and rationality. The "first cause" was the laws and wishes of God not found in religion but in nature. God was represented on earth through the order and harmony of nature. Reason was the only means of perfecting man and of initiating social change defined by the *philosophes.* Reason was a "universal critical intelligence" which, when coupled with human experience, should guide human action. Sentiment for the *philosophes* was their emotional reformism, which Carl Becker defined as "a mission to perform, a message to deliver to mankind; and to this messianic enterprise they brought an extraordinary amount of earnest conviction, of devotion, of enthusiasm."[37]

The *philosophes,* utilizing reason, developed a religion of humanity to replace all existing religions. The religion of humanity exalted the interests of mankind above those of one class, group, or even country. The *philosophes,* emphasizing the importance of humanity, sought to enlighten and improve the condition of the whole human race through a reaction against Christianity. This religion of humanity presumed that man was not innately depraved, that the end of life was not salvation but a good life on earth, that reason and experience should guide man in obtaining the good life, and that man's mind should be free from the ignorance and superstition inculcated by existing religions and society. Finally, the *philosophes'* concern with perfectibility focused on the perfectibility of man and society. For them, the human race was perfectible because nature shaped man.[38] Using his natural faculties it was possible for man to bring his ideas, conduct, and society in harmony with nature and the universal natural order.

Utilizing these seven concepts or suppositions about man, society, and nature, the *philosophes* developed both analyses of society and man and what was wrong with both, and prescriptions and programs for changing man and society to make both more consistent with nature. The *philosophes'* primary contention was that societal institutions repressed the true nature of man, altering man's perfect state by denying him his natural rights and the necessities for a physical, moral, and intellectual existence. In particular, Christianity and the personified God of Christianity distorted the simple and orderly processes of nature. Consequently, Christianity distorted the nature of man and society. Thus society, mainly due to the impact of religion on its structure, was divided into classes, groups, sects, and countries, which divided mankind. Religion-ruled society perceived of man as innately depraved and so believed that the end of life must be salvation after death rather than a good life on earth. An educational process that reflected the beliefs and divisions of religion inculcated man's mind with the superstitions of religion to the extent that man became unable to utilize and develop his reasoning capabilities.

The analysis of society that Wollstonecraft developed reflected these Enlightenment suppositions and analyses of society. Like the *philosophes*, Wollstonecraft conceived of nature as the earthly representation of God. "Nature," she stated, "or, so to speak with strict propriety, God, has made all things right."[39] But while the *philosophes* argued that society denied man his natural rights, Wollstonecraft, conceding this issue, asserted that the natural rights of man, emanating from nature, were denied woman throughout history. A woman in male society, she asserted, never had the opportunity to acquire these rights. Instead, "the rights of humanity have been thus confined to the male line from Adam downwards."[40] "But if women are to be excluded, without having a voice, from a participation of the natural rights of mankind, prove first, to ward off the charge of injustice and inconsistency, that they want reason."[41]

The perfect society for Wollstonecraft as for the *philosophes* was one in which God, or nature, and natural harmony and order became part of man's nature, so that man's own life reflected the harmony and order of nature. This required that man control his emotions and passions, ruling himself and society through reason— reason conceived of as a means of perfecting man and society.

Reason was, consequently, the simple power of improvement or, more properly speaking, of discerning truth.[42] "From the progress of reason, we be authorized to infer, that all governments will be meliorated, and the happiness of man placed on the solid basis."[43] In sum, reason, guided by experience, could perfect society.

Wollstonecraft's conclusions that emotion, not reason, controlled woman and that male-structured societal institutions, especially education, denied woman the opportunity to develop her reason obviously were part of her Enlightenment perspective. These conclusions ultimately led Wollstonecraft to believe that the development of woman's reason must have a higher priority than the *philosophes'* recommendations for man's improved reason. "I, therefore, will venture to assert," she stated, "that till women are more rationally educated, the progress of human virtue and improvement in knowledge must receive continual checks."[44]

Emphasizing the importance of reason for improving woman, Wollstonecraft, like the *philosophes,* criticized the divisions of humanity on earth perpetuated in particular by hereditary wealth and religion and recommended a religion of humanity in which reason and experience guide human actions. The individual, she believed with the *philosophes,* depended upon experience to develop his or her full faculties.

> The fact is, that men expect from education, what education cannot give. A sagacious parent or tutor may strengthen the body and sharpen the instruments by which the child is to gather knowledge; but the honey must be the reward of the individual's own industry. It is almost as absurd to attempt to make a youth wise by the experience of another, as to expect the body to grow strong by the exercise which is only talked of, or seen.[45]

This is important because, according to Wollstonecraft, woman could never obtain such experience. Because of her sex, woman could never be set free from superstition and emotion; nor would she ever possess a good life on earth.[46]

Then, one may ask, did Wollstonecraft believe that woman was *not* perfectible? At the outset, Wollstonecraft's analysis seemed to indicate that woman possessed too many disadvantages and restraints in society to develop her reason. But ultimately Wollstonecraft contended that woman could be perfected by bringing her conduct and life into accord with the natural harmony and order of nature, in rather the same process that the *philosophes* recommended for the improvement of man's capabilities.

Wollstonecraft was able to assert that woman was perfectible because she adopted Condillac's view of human development. First, "It is of great importance to observe that the character of every man is, in some degree, formed by his profession."[47] For woman as for man, society and the societal environment shaped character. But circumstances—especially those of woman's education—exerted a negative influence over woman that kept her emotional and passionate. Although woman was perfectible like man, initiating her improvement was a more difficult task than improving man, for all of society operated to perpetuate woman's lack of reason—including those men who were improved.

Thus Wollstonecraft's analysis of woman's status in society proceeded from the basic suppositions of Enlightenment philosophy about man, nature, God, society, reason, the religion of humanity, and human perfectibility. In her prescriptions and program for changing woman's status, Wollstonecraft utilized the same Enlightenment perspective.

The Enlightenment *philosophes* prescribed that society should change to provide each individual with the necessities for a physical, moral, and intellectual existence. Prerequisite to a moral and intellectual existence was the development of reason in each individual. Only a rational being could live a free, orderly existence in the *philosophes'* estimation. An individual should be guided by reason and experience and should be free of the divisive constraints imposed by Christian religions. The *philosophes* believed that man was ultimately perfectible. By using his reason, any man could purge himself of the erroneous notions resulting from education and religion.

The methods that the *philosophes* developed for instituting their prescriptions for a rational society and rational man were simplistic. While they assumed responsibility for enlightening the world about the religion of humanity, they believed that each individual should free himself. He should bring his ideas and conduct in harmony with nature by using his natural faculties and reason to expose errors in thought and structure in society and to purge his mind.

The responsibility for improving society and man resided, in other words, in the individual—once the *philosophes* showed the way.

Wollstonecraft agreed. Woman must possess the same natural rights as man, including, most importantly, rationality or reason, which she should develop and use in combination with experience to guide her life.

> Woman as well as man ought to have the common appetites and passions of their nature, they are only brutal when unchecked by reason; but the obligation to check them is the duty of mankind, not a sexual duty. Nature, in these respects, may safely be left to herself; let women only acquire knowledge and humanity, and love will teach them modesty.[48]

If society permitted woman to develop reason, as the *philosophes* recommended for man, then woman would be free and her nature would be consistent with the harmony and order of nature. Woman could be perfected.

The course that Wollstonecraft recommended for achieving woman's rationality was self-help. Like the *philosophes,* she believed that each individual must utilize his own faculties to perfect himself. Challenging women, Wollstonecraft said,

> If wisdom be desirable on its own account, if virtue to deserve the name must be founded on knowledge; let us endeavor to strengthen our minds, by reflection, till our heads become a balance for our hearts; let us not continue our thoughts to the petty occurrences of the day, or our knowledge to an acquaintance with our lovers' or husbands' hearts; but let the practice of every duty be subordinate to the grand one of improving our minds, and preparing our affections for a more exalted state.[49]

Yet Wollstonecraft recognized that woman in freeing herself confronted a more difficult task than man, for woman was *kept* unfree. Before woman could be truly free, the restrictions that man placed on woman must be removed, particularly governmental and educational restrictions. But whether or not the restrictions were removed, Wollstonecraft contended that woman should try to free herself through reason, for as the "enlightened" Wollstonecraft asserted, "They are free—who will be free!"[50]

Thus the feminist analysis that Wollstonecraft constructed in the *Vindication of the Rights of Woman* is, in conclusion, the basis of feminist ideology. Because of her Enlightenment perspective, Wollstonecraft gave to feminist ideology the same heritage that virtually all modern ideologies share—the Enlightenment. As Enlightenment thought influenced the development of socialism and liberal democracy, so it gave credence to and supported the development of feminist ideology.

Although it was not always warmly accepted in the 1790s and the early part of the nineteenth century in Britain and France, Mary Wollstonecraft's *Vindication* was at least well read. Especially the radical thinkers of the first quarter of the nineteenth century focused on the work as an expression of the rights and aspirations of a newly vocal group in society. The radicals most concerned with the woman's issue in this period were the utopian socialists, the Owenites in Britain and America and the Fourierists and Saint-Simonians in France.

UTOPIAN SOCIALIST FEMINISM

Utopian socialism evolved from the Enlightenment tradition in Europe in the late eighteenth century. Responding to the evolution of the Industrial Age and capitalism, the utopian socialists attempted to develop a new ideology about society and man's position within it based on the Enlightenment goals of rational man and society. Their objective was to restructure society in order to improve the condition and increase the happiness of all men.

As the Enlightenment tradition contributed to the development of a feminist ideology, so did utopian socialism. Within this tradition, two women predominated as contributors to the evolution of feminism as an ideology and to utopian socialism itself. Flora Tristan's *Promenades dans Londres* was a socialist interpretation of early nineteenth-century British society, and her *L'Union ouvrière* the first description in socialist literature of a syndicalist utopia. Tristan was most widely known for her association with the Fourierist movement in France, but she was also an ardent admirer of the socialists Robert Owen and Saint-Simon. She was a frequent participant in the group of political reformers and reformist theorists who sought to transform French society in the early part of the nineteenth century.[51] Tristan was, in summary, an important thinker in the utopian socialist tradition. As George Lichtheim concluded,

> The title of her book [L'Union ouvrière] was itself a program. It anticipated a good deal of the mature labor socialism of the next generation, and for all its naiveté, it had more immediate relevance than the elaborate schemes for economic planning worked out by writers like Louis Blanc.[52]

Frances Wright's position within the utopian socialist tradition was defined not so much by her treatises on socialism as by her activist attempts to institute socialist prescriptions. Wright was a close associate of Robert Dale Owen, the son of Robert Owen, and a participant in Robert Owen's New Harmony communitarian experiment in Indiana. After the collapse of New Harmony, Wright founded her own socialist utopia—Nashoba—in Tennessee. Nashoba was an attempt to institute an Owenite communitarian utopia for former American Negro slaves, with the goal of preparing them for life as free men. Although this experiment also quickly collapsed, Wright remained committed to her socialist vision. In a lecture delivered after the failure of Nashoba, entitled "On the Nature of Knowledge," she reiterated the Owenite belief in the formation of character by circumstances and the assimilation of "true" knowledge.

Both Wright and Tristan, thus, were important and active members of the utopian socialist movements of the early nineteenth century. Both developed utopian socialist analyses of society and prescriptions and programs for change which were integral parts of socialist ideology. But both Tristan's and Wright's ideological interests extended beyond utopian socialism to include feminism. In the *Promenades* and *L'Union*, Tristan included large sections on interpreting woman's status in society and methods and directions of change. Tristan planned a work on female equality that would have consolidated the feminist ideas in *Promenades* and *L'Union*. Unfortunately, she died before the work was written, although her notes were published posthumously by Alphonse Constant under the title *L'Émancipation de la Femme ou Testament de la Paria*. Frances Wright similarly was a vociferous exponent of woman's rights. Although she did not publish a treatise on feminist ideology per se, her letters and lectures were coherent expositions of woman's relationships to herself and society. Two collections of Wright's works reflect in particular the development of her feminist ideas: *Views of Society and Manners in America: in a Series of Letters from that Country to a Friend in England, During the Years 1818, 1819, and 1820* and *Course of Popular Lectures: With Three Addresses on Various Public Occasions, and a Reply to the Charges Against the French Reformers of 1789.*

While the feminist thought of both these theorists was not expressed in treatise form, as was Wollstonecraft's *Vindication,* they both still made significant contributions to the development of a feminist ideology. Drawing from socialist interpretations of and prescriptions for economic and social structures, Tristan and Wright significantly expanded the scope of the economic and social aspects of feminism only briefly mentioned by Wollstonecraft. They were not as concerned with the moral improvement of society and generic man as they were with the self-fulfillment and development of individual capabilities, more in line with a democratic concern for self-realization. Each discussed the situation of woman as part of the overall societal problems created or intensified by modern industrial society. In their analyses of woman's status in society and prescriptions and programs for change, therefore, both Wright and Tristan employed their utopian socialist perspectives.

Frances Wright and the Dawning of Utopia

Wright's analysis of women in American society was very similar to that of Wollstonecraft. She was both concerned with woman's performance in her role as mother and distressed at the fact that woman's lack of education and resultant ignorance made her unable to raise and educate her children adequately. In a lecture on "The Nature of Knowledge," Wright bemoaned woman's ignorance and its consequences.

> Think it not indifferent whether those who are to form the opinions, sway the habits, decide the destinies, of the species—and that not through their children only, but through their lovers and capricious

husbands—are enlightened friends or capricious mistresses, efficient coadjutors or careless servants, reasoning beings or blind followers of superstition.[53]

Wright's analysis of woman's lack of preparation for motherhood was, however, more broadly based than Wollstonecraft's. Her concern was political. While Wollstonecraft viewed mothers as incapable of teaching their children to be rational, Wright concluded that mothers cannot teach citizenship and knowledge of self-government. "In a country where a mother is charged with the formation of the infant mind that is to be called in the future to judge of the laws and support the liberties of a republic, the mother herself should well understand those laws, and estimate those liberties."[54]

Another similarity between Wollstonecraft and Wright was their fear that unless woman developed her intellectual capabilities, the human race would not progress. Again, Wright's analysis was broader than Wollstonecraft's. Wollstonecraft was concerned about the rational development of the race. Unless woman was rational and virtuous, the human race as a whole would not acquire virtue. For Wright, human progress included, but was not limited to, rational and moral development. Wright's analysis focused more on the relationship and performance of the individual in society—on his or her exercise of power. The human race would only progress if woman developed intellectually (became rational, in Wollstonecraft's terms) and morally and then exercised her newly found intellect to better society.

It is in vain that we would circumscribe the power of one half of our race, and that half by far the most important and most influential. If they exert it not for good, they will for evil; if they advance not knowledge, they will perpetuate ignorance. Let women stand where they may on the scale of improvement, their position decides that of the race. Are they cultivated, so is society polished and enlightened. Are they ignorant?—so is it gross and insipid. Are they wise?—so is the human condition prosperous. Are they foolish?—so is it unstable and unpromising. Are they free?—so is the human character elevated. Are they enslaved?—so is the whole race degraded.[55]

At this point the similarities between the ideas of Wollstonecraft and Wright end. While Wright, for example, criticized the lack of education for woman, as did Wollstonecraft, she did so for very different reasons. Wright believed that woman's lack of education deprived her of equal rights and freedom with men in society. "Equal rights! they cannot exist without equality of instruction."[56] Thus, while Wright also inherited the Enlightenment tradition and its emphasis on moral and rational development, her criticisms of woman's existing status in society were focused more politically than those of Wollstonecraft. The democratic ideals of political power, equal rights, and freedom of the individual were Wright's primary criteria for evaluating woman's status. Woman performed her motherhood role poorly because she lacked political knowledge and could not teach her children citizenship. Woman's lack of education rendered her incapable of being free or obtaining equal rights. The human race would not progress because woman lacked political power.

When analyzing the causes of woman's inferior status, Wright's interpretation began to deviate strongly from Wollstonecraft's analysis. Drawing heavily upon the Owenite distrust and hatred of religion, Wright discredited religion as a moral force in society. Like the Owenites, Wright distinguished between established religions and the concept of religion in general, that is, religion as a moral-ethical ideal. Wright defined the religion she abhorred as follows. "Religion, as distinguished from morals, may be defined thus: *a belief in, and homage rendered to, existences unseen and causes unknown.*"[57]

In Wright's feminist analysis, religion was the primary cause of woman's unequal stature in society. Religion rendered woman inferior because the priesthood controlled government by influencing the male population, and the priesthood's "very subsistence depends, of necessity, upon the mental and moral degradation of their fellow creatures."[58] Religion consequently subjugated woman by undermining her reason with myths and "phantoms."[59] While men tyrannized woman, they themselves were tyrannized by the priesthood. They were no more free than woman to reason and act as free agents. In politics and society, men were the mere lackeys of the priesthood, and male dominance over woman was taught and maintained through the tyranny of religion.

Given this socialist-feminist analysis of woman's status in society and the factors that suppress her, Wright's prescriptions for woman's future roles and programs for achieving these prescriptions were both clearly defined and wide-ranging. In this part of her analysis, Wright made her most significant contributions to the development of feminist ideology. Wright believed that woman's stature could not be altered unless society as a whole underwent dramatic change. And so her prescriptions affected society in its entirety.

Wright first prescribed that absolute equality should exist in society, not merely equality between man and woman, but also equality among classes and races. "Were the vital principle of human equality universally acknowledged, it would be to my fellow beings without regard to nation, class, sect, or sex, that I should delight to address myself."[60] Prerequisite for such broad-based society equality was an equal system of education. Equal education was not only necessary to achieve equal rights for all in society, but without it a republican or democratic government could not exist. Equal education, then, was the basis for a free society and free individuals in society, including women. Wright's ultimate prescription was for "practical equality, or, the universal and equal improvement of the condition of all."[61]

While in her prescriptions Wright focused generally upon improving the condition of all oppressed groups in society, she also outlined specific changes to benefit women. For instance, she advocated equal property rights in marriage, an issue on which she first focused in 1829.[62] In an article in *The Free Enquirer*, March 5, 1831, she expanded her prescriptions for woman to include birth control and more liberal divorce laws. Wright advocated birth control because she thought it evil to bring children into the world who could not be properly cared for. The only remedy for such an evil lay with restricting the size of families. Wright similarly urged the passage of liberal divorce laws so that the unhappily wed could be easily separated.[63] Wright, then, called for broad-based and far-sighted social, political, and legal change that would improve and equalize the status of woman in society. These changes far surpassed Wollstonecraft's advocacy of equal education for woman to make her a more rational and better wife and mother.

Wright's courses of action for achieving her prescriptions, both general and specific, also extended far beyond Wollstonecraft's analysis. They included specific policy guidelines in addition to general directions of change. It is important to note, however, that Wright's strategies were seldom limited to concrete actions for woman. Her concern was not that narrow. Wright instead focused on strategies to improve society as a whole and all of the groups within it, of which women were only one.

Wright's first course was to eliminate religion as it existed in her day, replacing it with a science of morals. "Let, then, morals, or *the science of human life,* assume, among a people boasting themselves free, (and free, rightly interpreted, would mean *rational*) the place of religion."[64] This "science of morals" was a socialist, particularly an Owenite, interpretation and adaptation of Bentham's utilitarian pleasure/pain principle.

> In considering the science of morals, it might seem, at the first glance, to divide itself into two distinct heads: as our conduct affects ourselves, and as it affects others. This distinction, however, is more apparent than real, since it is barely possible for us to consider any action, much less any course of actions, without a reference to their effects, either immediate or more remote, by example, on the sentient beings around us; which effects must ever again react upon ourselves, and influence, pleasurably or painfully, our state of being.[65]

"In this preference of others to self, or, to put it according to the views of the moralists before quoted, *in this seeking of our own pleasure through the pleasure of others,* consists the highest degree of active virtue."[66]

In addition to eliminating existing religions, Wright advocated the acquisition of just knowledge and the cultivation of reason as methods for improving society. "It is equally our interest and our duty, to aim at the acquisition of just knowledge, with a view to the formation of just opinions."[67] Just knowledge and reason could be obtained only through a revised system of education in which all sexes, classes, and races were educated equally. In her advocacy of equal education, Wright outlined a detailed, concrete, national system of education that regulated the content, structure, and administration of education for both males and females. Of fundamental importance for Wright was that males and females should be raised equally. Such equal treatment could only be achieved by state regulated schools.[68]

I would suggest that the state legislatures be directed (after laying off the whole in townships or hundreds) to organize, at suitable distances, and in convenient and healthy situations, establishments for the general reception of all children resident within the said school district. These establishments to be devoted, severally, to children between a certain age. Say, the first, infants between two and four, or two and six; according to the density of the population, and such other local circumstances as might render a greater or less number of establishments necessary or practicable. The next to receive children from four to eight, or six to twelve years. The next from twelve to sixteen, or an older age if found desirable. Each establishment to be furnished with instructors with all the apparatus, land, and conveniences necessary for the best development of all knowledge; the same, whether operative or intellectual, being always calculated to the age and strength of the pupils.[69]

Wright's most important recommendation for equalizing the positions of male and female, classes and races in society was, therefore, education. She emphasized that a changed system of education was a prerequisite for other societal changes.

Wright, as we have seen, delineated both specific prescriptions for change in society and programs for achieving these prescriptions. These changes were to be implemented through governmental action. "Let the industrious class, and all honest men of all classes, unite for a gradual, but radical reform, in all the objects, and all the measure of government; and let this be done through, and by the means supplied in their constitutional code: namely—*through their legislature.*"[70] Wright's strategy was simple. Let society democratize itself democratically.

This strategy of legislative change unfortunately had several difficulties with implementation that Wright failed to consider. For example, Wright proposed that a national system of education should be instituted to allow society to obtain "just knowledge" and reason. She claimed that in society as it existed men possessed distorted knowledge and that they were manipulated by the priesthood. Yet she offered no solution to the resultant dilemma of how legislatures, themselves corrupted by the priesthood and unjust knowledge, would obtain the freedom from prejudice and foresight and insight to establish such a system of education. Secondly, if men were manipulated by religion, if religion molded their behavior and thoughts, how could they be stimulated to abolish religion and replace it with a science of morals? In other words, while Wright realized that reform must be gradual when she said, "Great reforms are not wrought in a day. Evils which are the accumulated results of accumulated errors, are not to be struck down at a blow by the nod of a magician,"[71] she failed to identify a starting point for implementing her changes. Unlike the other utopian socialists, she did not consider herself an enlightened prophet who would lead the way for society. Nor after the failure of her Nashoba community did she believe that communitarian environments would enlighten society. So, while her strategies for changing society, including the status of woman, were far more developed than Wollstonecraft's, Wright failed to consider the issue of how to motivate unenlightened legislators to legislate enlightened policies.

Flora Tristan: A Moderate Socialist's View of Woman

Flora Tristan's contributions to the development of a feminist ideology were made generally after Frances Wright gained prominence in America and Britain as an advocate of female equality. Yet, ideologically, Tristan fell somewhere between Wollstonecraft and Wright, especially in her analysis of woman's status and her prescriptions for societal change. Her contributions to feminist thought, therefore, were not very significant, despite her profound impact on British and especially French intellectual circles. She was an active participant in the developing feminist intellectual fervor in Europe in the early nineteenth century. She read and analyzed Wollstonecraft's *Vindication* and considered Wollstonecraft's prescriptions for female equality revolutionary. She met and discussed feminism with Anna Wheeler, a British Owenite feminist, and with leading socialists of her time, such as Owen and Fourier.[72] Therefore, while Tristan was an important socialist and feminist in the socialist movements of the early nineteenth century in France and England, her contributions to the evolution of feminist ideology were not particularly innovative, although several of her analyses expanded the scope of feminist thought.

In her criticisms of woman's status in society, Tristan struck a comfortable medium between Wollstonecraft and Wright. Wollstonecraft was overly concerned with the wifely and motherly roles of woman, and her prescriptions and programs for change consequently were narrowly developed. They failed to consider needed economic and political reforms. Wright, in contrast, over-emphasized her Owenite preoccupation with the detrimental effects of religion on woman, man, and society in her criticisms of woman's role. Her conclusion that religion was the primary cause of all social ills, including woman's inferiority, necessarily resulted in her recommendation of abolishing religion, a virtually impossible task.

Tristan's analysis reconciled the Enlightenment preoccupation with rational development and the socialist hatred of religion. For Tristan as for Wollstonecraft, woman was romantic and naive. She stated in the *Promenades,* "The imagination of the young female takes a romantic direction."[73] Also like Wollstonecraft, she blamed woman's lack of education for depriving her of rationality and making her a creature of prejudice. "They are noble and grand in manners; but alas! all of their innate good qualities are suffocated by a system of education founded on false principles and by an atmosphere of hypocrisy, prejudices, and vices that surrounds their life."[74]

Tristan, however, did not limit her criticisms to education alone. Religion was also an important factor. Religion affected women deleteriously, not through its manipulation of the male population (as Wright argued) but because it made woman's education primarily scriptural and religious.[75] Woman's education prepared her neither to educate her children properly, a concern for both Wollstonecraft and Wright, nor to assume civil and political rights.

A major concern for Tristan which neither Wright nor Wollstonecraft focused on was prostitution. In the *Promenades dans Londres* Tristan devoted considerable attention to a discussion of prostitution in an attempt to understand the phenomenon. She reached no concrete conclusions about prostitution, although she hypothesized that it was a consequence both of woman's inability to support herself adequately economically and of the examples of prostitution that the Bible taught. She concluded her analysis by stating, "The prostitute is for me an unpenetrable mystery. . . . she is the fiancee of pain, devoted to humiliation—physical tortures incessantly repeated—moral death every instant—and *contempt for herself.*"[76]

Like Wollstonecraft and Wright, Tristan's recommendations for improving woman's status in society included improving woman's education, consequently allowing the individual to develop more fully, and establishing absolute equality for woman. "It is necessary, therefore, that women, in particular women of the masses, collect in their infancy a rational, solid education, proper to develop all of the good inclinations that are in them."[77] This emphasis on rational education evolved from Tristan's concern that woman should be adequately prepared to educate her children. Tristan, like Wright, extended her prescriptions further than Wollstonecraft, stressing that all classes of women, not merely the middle class, should be educated properly.

Of primary concern for Tristan, though, was that woman should acquire absolute equality with man—civil, political, economic, and religious. "They should be accorded absolute equality with man first in pursuance of their legal rights which should be employed from infancy, but also because the oversight of this equality has caused all the miseries of the world."[78] In this attempt to justify woman's right to equality, Tristan made the first feminist argument in support of female *superiority* in some areas of intellect. For Tristan as for the ideologists who followed her, woman possessed greater and more fully developed instinctual and intuitive powers than man. "Woman, in effect, reflects the divine light; she possesses a higher degree of intuition than man."[79]

In conclusion, Tristan's analysis of woman's status in society and her prescriptions for changing this status generally were reiterations of the earlier feminists Wollstonecraft and Wright. Her importance for the development of feminist ideology was her concern over prostitution and her arguments for female superiority in some areas. Particularly the idea of a unique feminine intellect, somewhat more developed than male intellect, was adopted and stressed as fundamentally important by later feminists. Tristan's prescriptions, like those of Wright, reflected her socialist identification. She advocated the implementation of workers' unions in which all individuals, regardless of class, sex, or race, would be equal civilly, politically, economically, and educationally. Tristan, however, provided even fewer programs than Wright for implementing her socialist utopia.

The feminist thought of Tristan and Wright unequivocally was derived from a utopian socialist perspective. When they deviated from or contributed to the feminist ideas of Mary Wollstonecraft, the differences were a consequence of their socialism. While utopian socialism as an ideology was a composite of the thought of a variety of ideologists from diverse backgrounds, the most important ideologists were Robert Owen, Henri Saint-Simon, and Charles Fourier. Of these three, both Wright and Tristan more closely approximated the ideology of Owen, and in fact openly acknowledged his influence upon their thought.

Utopian Socialism and Feminism

Utopian socialism in general proceeded from the underlying principles of Enlightenment thought, especially the concept of rationality or reason. The principle of rationality was vital to the utopians for understanding man's and society's true natures. Owen stated, "Consistency in thought and action constitutes that which is rational. . . . inconsistency of ideas and actions is the character of irrationality."[80] In their socialist treatises, both Wright and Tristan reflected the utopian socialists' belief in rationality and the conclusion that irrationality prevailed in the new industrial world. They utilized Owen's analysis that rationality for all people was important and that societal circumstances controlled the development of rationality and reason. As Wright concluded, "Let us cast aside fear and suspicion, suspend our jealousies and disputes, acknowledge the rights of others and assert our own. And oh! let us understand that the first and noblest of these rights is the cultivation of our reason."[81] Wright and Tristan agreed that man was perfectible. When provided with the correct societal circumstances, every individual could become rational and happy. "Then one would understand that the law of humanity is continued progress; its condition, perfectibility."[82]

The utopian socialists, and Owen in particular, analyzed society and the individual's position in society in terms of this belief in man's rationality and the formation of character. Seven features of industrial capitalism, according to Owen, were necessarily irrational and hence hindered man's rational development. These were individualism, laissez-faire capitalism, the means and modes of production in capitalist society, religion, private property, marriage and family structures, and education. Wright and Tristan both cited the same seven causes of irrationality.

Individualism, Owen argued, created irrationality in society because it divided mankind into economic, political, and social classes and spheres. "From the principle of individual self-interest have arisen all the divisions of mankind, the endless errors and mischiefs of class, sect, party, and national antipathies, creating the malevolent passions, and all the crimes and misery with which the human race have been hitherto afflicted."[83] Wright and Tristan also vehemently criticized the individualism prevalent in society. As Tristan concluded, "the narrow individualism of the English is the cause of their curse."[84]

Laissez-faire capitalism created divisions between mankind—the development of wealthy classes and the differentiation of workers and owners. Centralized control of the means of production prevented workers from accumulating even the necessities of life. Their achievement of happiness was thus hindered because they lacked the time to develop their natural faculties and to become rational.

The means and modes of production of industrial capitalism, which required long hours and bad working conditions in factories, increased the irrationality of man, woman, and child because they denied opportunities for other pursuits, such as education or recreation. The lack of education and the stifling conditions of the factories destroyed children's intellectual capabilities before they had begun to develop. The division of labor, by which a person performed only one part of a creative task, destroyed the harmony of any worker's nature. Because the products of labor possessed no identifiable personal value to the worker, he lacked pride in himself and his product. "There is the most minute division of mental power and manual labor in the individuals of the working classes, private interests are placed perpetually at variance with the public good."[85] Wright and Tristan especially emphasized that the worker never received the full value of his labor. A member of the working class barely earned a subsistence existence, while he made the owners of the means of production wealthy. "The hardest labour is often without a reward adequate to the sustenance of the labourer . . .

whose patient, sedulous industry supplies the community with all its comforts, and the rich with all their luxuries."[86]

Of all the causes of irrationality that Owen and the utopian socialists identified in society, religion was the social institution that received the most criticism. Owen offered an even more cogent criticism of religion than Wright.

It is true that religions have been and to this day are the strongest causes of repulsive feelings between individuals and nations; and while any of these deranging systems of the human intellect shall be forced into the young mind by the insane contending sects over the world, the spirit of universal charity and love must remain unknown among all nations and peoples.[87]

The private ownership of industry, goods, and homes, combined with the unequal opportunity to accumulate wealth, reinforced the alienation of men, according to Owen and the utopian socialists. Intellectually, private property destroyed man's character. Instead of teaching man that his happiness depended on the happiness of others, it instilled greed, vanity, and pride. Man became self-interested and concerned with his own advancement in society to the detriment of those around him. Private property not only created the inequality of condition that existed between men in industrial capitalist society, it also inculcated within man the valuing of inequality. As Wright observed, "the estimate of our own moral and political importance swelling always in a ratio exactly proportioned to the growth of our purse."[88]

The institutions of marriage and the family also created inequality of condition between people. Marriage and the family set people against each other. For Owen, Wright, and Tristan alike, in the family relationship the husband was the intellectual, physical, and moral ruler of the wife and children. Consequently, wife and children were unable to develop their own potential as human beings or to create their own happiness.[89]

Finally, the existing systems of education were criticized by the utopian socialists because they taught and reinforced the perceived value of all previously discussed causes of irrationality. Rather than encouraging individuals to develop their own potential and creativity and rather than teaching individuals that their own happiness depended on the happiness of others, education reinforced the values of industrial capitalism, private property, wealth, and individualism and supported the existing religions of the world. As Wright concluded, education, by being "equally false and deficient, and . . . full of falacies, theories, and hypotheses"[90] and too scripturally oriented, reinforced societal circumstances and institutions detrimental to the development of rationality, happiness, and harmony.[91]

Thus, for the utopian socialists, including Wright and Tristan, man was a product of his environment. He was created by the circumstances that surrounded him. The existing circumstances of the world inhibited the development of his rationality so that he lived by irrationality and emotion. Because each individual's character was not correctly formed, society perpetuated man's irrationality and unhappiness through incorrect social and economic circumstances.

While the utopian socialists concerned themselves primarily with society in general, all utopian socialists also focused on woman's particular condition within society. Owen described woman's unique condition of oppression in criticizing marriage and the family. Fourier, however, developed a more explicit analysis of woman's status in society and concluded that ameliorating woman's societal condition was a prerequisite for improving society as a whole. The feminist utopian socialists utilized and expanded Fourier's analysis of woman.

Fourier was, as George Lichtheim observed, "indeed a radical feminist and an advocate of complete equality between the sexes."[92] Fourier, like Owen, opposed the institution of marriage because it encouraged male egotism and social atomization, relegating woman to the status of housekeeper at the cost of the proper development of her natural talents. But unlike Owen, Fourier identified woman's societal condition as a key for understanding the oppression of all people in society and as a criterion for measuring societal improvement. Woman's subjection for Fourier was part of a cultural process in which the relatively free and equal, albeit primitive, people of ancient society were divided into classes. Woman in this development of class society became classless, lacking a class identity. Woman was the group in society to which all men were superior.

Societal progress, thus, was best measured and evaluated by the improvement of woman's societal condition. The freer woman was from oppression, the freer male-oriented social classes would become. As Fourier stated,

> The change in historical epochs can always be determined by the progress of woman toward freedom, because in the relation of woman to man, of the weak to the strong, the victory of human nature over brutality is the most evident. The degree of feminine emancipation is the natural measure of general emancipation.[93]

The criticisms of woman's status in society that both Wright and Tristan developed evolved from their socialist criticisms of society in general and from an expansion of Fourier's and Owen's criticisms of woman's status. Yet their analyses of woman's status were very narrow compared to their socialist analyses of society. When evaluating woman's societal status, Wright and Tristan utilized primarily the concepts and criteria that Wollstonecraft employed from her Enlightenment perspective, those concepts and criteria that the Enlightenment *philosophes* and the utopian socialists held in common—rationality, reason, and critiques of religion, education, and marriage.

Both Wright and Tristan were most concerned about woman's lack of rationality in industrial capitalist society. Because woman was part of the irrational human race, she too was irrational. Like Wollstonecraft and Fourier, they concluded that because woman lacked rationality, the human race itself suffered. Wright in particular developed an analysis of the relationship between woman's irrationality and inequality similar to that of Fourier. As she observed, "let women stand where they may in the scale of improvement, their position decides that of the race."[94]

In identifying the specific factors in society that perpetuated woman's irrationality, Wright and Tristan delineated three overwhelmingly important societal institutions—religion, education, and the family. Because religion controlled society and the religions of the world believed in woman's inferiority, Wright concluded that woman was relegated to inequality. While Tristan more closely approximated Wollstonecraft's analysis of religion's detrimental influence on woman—that it functioned predominantly through educational systems—she also admitted that religion, and especially the leaders of organized religions, encouraged woman's inferiority throughout society. In their analyses of education's detrimental influence on woman, Wright and Tristan very closely approximated Wollstonecraft's positions that woman's education was unequal to man's because of its scriptural orientation, and that if woman was to be a good wife and mother she must have an equal education. Lastly, Wright and Tristan, like Wollstonecraft and the utopian socialists, criticized woman's inequality in the institutions of marriage and the family. "She is a thing, a furnishing," Tristan observed. "The husband commands, sees to their affairs, keeping his woman outside of these decisions; he wastes the dowry without which his spouse is enslaved, borrowing from it to defend their interests."[95]

Wright and Tristan obviously developed analyses of woman from their utopian socialist perspectives. They did not contribute to the development of feminist ideology, however, because those components of utopian socialism that they employed to analyze woman's status in society were the beliefs and values first asserted by Wollstonecraft and the Enlightenment tradition. Yet, while the socialist perspectives of Wright and Tristan did not contribute to the development of feminism's critique of woman's status in society, the prescriptions and strategies they developed for changing woman's status in society clearly did. They applied to woman's condition purely socialist recommendations for changing society. Their contributions to the development of feminist ideology were the social, economic, educational, and religious changes that they prescribed and the programs suggested to implement these changes.

At base, the utopian socialists prescribed a rational society. But because they believed that environment shaped man, society must become rational. In a rational society, each part of man's nature—physical, moral, and intellectual—should be fully developed and in harmony with nature. In a rational state of society, all competition and divisiveness between men should cease. All men should be equal.

In developing programs for achieving the rational state of society, the utopian socialists outlined both short- and long-term courses of action. Short-term reforms sought to ameliorate the condition of man in society and, in particular, the working classes. The long-term objective of the utopian socialists, however, involved a total restructuring of society along communitarian lines. Specifically, the utopian socialists recommended religious, economic, political, and educational changes.

Their first recommendation was for the abolition of all existing religions. In the place of religion, the utopians suggested a "rational religion," a return to the humanist teachings of Christ. Economically, industrial capitalism should be replaced, at first by a period of "state socialism." Until the working classes achieved educational equality with the upper and middle classes, a benevolent state must devise legislative measures to benefit all of society. Initially the state must replace the capitalist standard of value with a natural standard of value based on the amount of labor exerted in production. For the unemployed, the state should provide national employment, or, in contemporary terminology, public works projects. In brief, the state must insure that each individual in society acquired the physical necessities of life.

Perhaps the most significant strategy that the utopian socialists developed for changing society to benefit all of mankind was their system of education. Education should be available to and equal for all people in society. Owen proposed a free, national system of education. The purpose of this national system was to transform irrational man and woman into rational human beings by cultivating and equalizing the three parts of human nature.[96]

The ultimate goal of these political, economic, educational, and religious changes in society was the goal of all the utopian socialists— a communitarian structure of society. Owen called his communities "parallelograms." Fourier named them "phalanstères." But the concept of both systems was the same. Society should be divided into small communities with agriculturally based economies. In this type of society, individuals would be surrounded with rational circumstances. These communities were the long-term strategies of the utopian socialists.

The feminist socialists Wright and Tristan employed both short- and long-term programs of the utopian socialists to define prescriptions and strategies for improving woman's status. They simply contended that if society in general was restructured along socialist lines, then woman's condition in society necessarily would improve. Like the other utopian socialists, Wright and Tristan advocated the establishment of a rational society. In this rational society all people would be equal, including "absolute equality of men and women."[97] As short-term strategies for changing society and woman's condition, both feminists, as we have discussed, prescribed educational, religious, economic, and marital changes.

The influence of Wright's socialist perspective on her feminist thought was most pronounced in her recommendation of a national system of education whose content, structure, and administration should be determined by the state. Tristan also emphasized the importance of a rational system of education, especially for woman. "It is necessary, then, that women, in particular working class women, receive in their childhood a rational, solid education, proper to develop all of the good inclinations that are in them."[98] Wright and Tristan recommended abolishing the organized religions of the world, which they identified as detrimental to cooperation in society. Religion should be replaced by a "science of morals" for Wright that closely resembled Owen's rational religion. And lastly, in discussing changes within the marriage relationship, Tristan and especially Wright advocated a complete alteration in the legal basis of the marriage relationship and hence contributed to the development of feminist thought. Wright attempted to delineate an egalitarian marriage relationship based on equal legal and property rights for woman. A married woman must be permitted to own property. Perhaps more importantly, a woman should be allowed freedom within the marriage relationship—the freedom to have or not have children, that is, birth control, the freedom of divorce on an equal basis with man, and the freedom to control her own property. The conditions within the marriage relationship outlined by Owen and Fourier would be resolved at least in part by the marriage relationship described by the feminists.

Only one major difference between the utopian socialists and the feminist socialists existed for changing society. Both groups identified the same economic problems in society and recommended better means and modes of production and the elimination of economic classes. But the feminists disagreed with their mentors over whether economic change should be a long- or short-term goal. Both Fourier and Owen defined a long-term strategy of complete economic change via the establishment of an agricultural communitarian society. Owen, in addition, defined concrete, short-term proposals for ameliorating the worst conditions of society—changes in wage standards, public employment, improvement in working conditions—to be accomplished through a system of state socialism legislating remedies.

Tristan rejected the development of communities as unfeasible. Instead, she proposed a system of workers' unions whose purposes would be to give workers economic power and to permit them to improve their own societal condition. This system would include women as equal participants in determining economic policy. Wright's program for economic change was antithetical to the other utopian socialists. As a first stage, she suggested and attempted to institute communitarianism as a means for changing economic relationships in society. After the failure of her Nashoba community, however, Wright altered her proposed strategies for economic change. Instead of communities, she adopted legislative action as a long-term program, arguing that it would be the best way to transform society economically and to provide woman with economic equality.[99]

In summary, Wright and Tristan in the prescriptions and especially the programs they developed for changing society along socialist lines contributed significantly to the development of feminist thought. Implicit in their socialist recommendations was the assumption that woman's status would automatically improve once society became more socialistic. The quest of the utopian socialists for complete equality of every individual, including women, became part of feminist thought through the ideas of Wright and Tristan. But the utopian socialists and the feminist socialists alike saw the need for special changes in society to equalize woman's status. These changes included a freedom within marriage in terms of legal and property rights and an economic freedom for woman implicit in a socialist society. These recommendations—equality in marriage and the workplace—were the significant additions to feminist thought made by Wright and Tristan. They laid the basis for the development of feminist ideology.

NOTES

1. William Godwin, *Memoirs of Mary Wollstonecraft*, ed. W. Clark Durant (New York: Gordon Press, 1972), p. 67.

2. Ibid., p. xxxvii.

3. Janet Todd, Introduction to Mary Wollstonecraft, *An Historical and Moral View of the Origin and Progress of the French Revolution and the Effect It Has Produced in Europe*, 2nd ed. (London: J. Johnson, 1795), pp. 6-7.

4. Godwin, *Memoirs*, pp. xxx-xxxiii.

5. Ibid., pp. 56-57.

6. Mary Wollstonecraft, *A Vindication of the Rights of Woman* (1792; reprint ed., New York: W.W. Norton and Company, 1967), p. 73.

7. Ibid., p. 97.

8. Ibid., p. 104.

9. Ibid., p. 151.

10. Ibid., p. 101.

11. Ibid., p. 213.

12. Ibid., p. 216.

13. Ibid., p. 227.

14. Ibid., pp. 49-50.

15. Ibid., p. 82.

16. Ibid., pp. 134-35.

17. Ibid., pp. 53-54.

18. Ibid., pp. 105-06.

19. Ibid., p. 124.

20. Ibid., p. 94.

21. Ibid., pp. 126-27.

22. Ibid., p. 216.

23. Ibid., p. 273.

24. Ibid., p. 70.

25. Ibid., p. 50.

26. Ibid., pp. 96-97.

27. Ibid., pp. 116-17.

28. Ibid., p. 258.

29. Ibid., p. 75.

30. Ibid., p. 72.

31. Ibid., pp. 158-59.

32. Ibid., p. 218.

33. Ibid., p. 263.

34. Ibid., p. 81.

35. Ibid., p. 138.

36. Ibid., p. 220.

37. Carl L. Becker, *The Heavenly City of the Eighteenth-Century Philosophers* (New Haven: Yale University Press, 1932), p. 43.

38. The *philosophes*, however, disagreed on their interpretations of perfectibility and human nature. Locke, for example, thought of man as

autonomous. Condillac, on the other hand, emphasized that man's mind became whatever the omnipotent environment made it.

39. Wollstonecraft, *Vindication*, p. 63.

40. Ibid., p. 141.

41. Ibid., p. 26.

42. Ibid., p. 94.

43. Wollstonecraft, *French Revolution*, p. 69.

44. Wollstonecraft, *Vindication*, p. 77.

45. Ibid., p. 175.

46. Ibid., p. 217.

47. Ibid., p. 46.

48. Ibid., p. 197.

49. Ibid., p. 147.

50. Ibid., p. 159.

51. Jean Baelen, *La vie de Flora Tristan: Socialisme et féminisme au 19ᵉ siècle* (Paris: Editions du Seuil, 1972), p. 115.

52. George Lichtheim, *The Origins of Socialism* (New York: Frederick A. Praeger, 1969), p. 70.

53. Frances Wright D'Arusmont, *Life, Letters and Lectures: 1834/1844* (New York: Arno Press, 1972), p. 32.

54. Frances Wright D'Arusmont, *Views of Society and Manners in America; in a Series of Letters From That Country to a Friend in England, During the Years 1818, 1819, and 1820* (London: Longman, Hurst, Rees, Orme, and Brown, 1812), p. 421.

55. D'Arusmont, *Life*, p. 24.

56. Ibid., p. 25.

57. Ibid., p. 73.

58. Ibid., preface, p. vii.

59. Ibid., p. 20.

60. Ibid., p. 20.

61. Ibid., p. 216.

62. Frances Wright, *The Free Enquirer*, April 29, 1829, quoted in William Randall Waterman, *Frances Wright* (New York: AMS Press, 1967).

63. Waterman, *Frances Wright*, p. 158.

64. D'Arusmont, *Life*, p. 153.

65. Ibid., p. 77.

66. Ibid., p. 80.

67. Ibid., p. 5.

68. Ibid., pp. 217-18.

69. Ibid., p. 116.

70. Ibid., p. 178.

71. Ibid., p. 109.

72. Baelen, *Tristan*, p. 30.

73. Flora Tristan, *Promenades dans Londres* (Paris: H.L. Delloye, 1840), p. 307, translated by Judith A. Sabrosky.

74. Ibid., p. 302.

75. Ibid., p. 306.

76. Ibid., p. 110.

77. Flora Tristan, quoted in Jules L. Puech, *La vie et l'oeuvre de Flora Tristan, 1803-1844* (Paris: Librairie Marcel Rivière et Cie, 1925), p. 351, translated by Judith A. Sabrosky.

78. Ibid.

79. Ibid., p. 356.

80. Robert Owen, *The Book of the New Moral World*, Part 1 (London: The Home Colonization Society, 1842), p. 35.

81. D'Arusmont, *Life*, p. 37.

82. Tristan, quoted in Baelen, p. 179, translated by Judith A. Sabrosky.

83. Robert Owen, "Report to the County of Lanark, 1820," in *The Life of Robert Owen, Written by Himself*, 2 vols. (London: Frank Cass & Co., Ltd., 1965), Ia: 285.

84. Tristan, quoted in Puech, *Flora Tristan*, p. 101.

85. Owen, "Lanark," p. 274.

86. D'Arusmont, *Life*, p. 108.

87. Owen, *Life*, I: 101.

88. D'Arusmont, *Life*, p. 111.

89. Robert Owen, *Lectures on an Entire New State of Society* (London: J. Brooks, 1830), p. 82.

90. D'Arusmont, *Life*, p. 9.

91. Tristan, *Promenades*, p. 306.

92. Lichtheim, *Socialism*, p. 35.

93. Charles Fourier, "Theorie des quatre mouvements," *Oeuvres Complètes*, p. 195.

94. D'Arusmont, *Life*, p. 42.

95. Tristan, *Promenades*, p. 141.

96. Robert Owen, *A New View of Society and Other Writings*, ed. G.D.H. Cole (New York: E.P. Dutton & Co., 1927), p. 74.

97. Tristan, *Promenades*, p. 353.

98. Tristan, quoted in Puech, *Flora Tristan*, p. 351.

99. D'Arusmont, *Life*, p. 178.

Feminist Ideology in the Nineteenth Century

WHILE THE FIRST FEMINIST analyses developed within intellectual traditions native to Europe, the real solidification of feminist ideas into an ideology occurred in the United States. The contributions to feminist ideology by American women in the first half of the nineteenth century encompassed both the most practical and the most philosophical components of feminist ideology. These contributions also emanated from uniquely American political and intellectual movements, although the indirect influence of European ideologies and philosophies on their development cannot be ignored. The groups from which the first true feminist ideology evolved were the Abolitionists and the Transcendentalists.

During the period in which Frances Wright was lecturing on female equality in the United States and Flora Tristan was publicizing feminism among socialist intellectuals in Europe, an American feminist published a set of lectures on feminism that far surpassed in analytical sophistication any previous feminist analysis. Sarah Grimké, best known for her work as an Abolitionist, published a series of letters in 1838 entitled *Letters on the Equality of the Sexes, and the Condition of Woman, Addressed to Mary S. Parker, President of the Boston Female Anti-Slavery Society.* In *Letters*, Grimké's analysis encompassed and expanded all the criticisms made of woman's status in society by earlier feminists. She was the first feminist to counter male arguments supporting female inferiority by proving the arguments false themselves. While she failed to expand the scope of feminist analyses, when she concisely coalesced the different European feminist ideas and applied them specifically to women in the United State, Grimké significantly increased the depth of these analyses.

Margaret Fuller, the Transcendentalist, fell at the opposite end of the philosophical spectrum from Grimké. While Grimké concerned herself with the practical consequences of inequality for woman, Fuller, in *Woman in the Nineteenth Century*, focused on the philosophical justifications for woman's equality and prescriptions and programs for instituting change. For the first time in the history of feminist ideology, Fuller constructed a philosophical analysis, instead of a factual documentation, of woman's societal and human conditions. In her concern with identifying the effects of inequality on woman's nature, Fuller established the philosophical bases of feminist ideology.

If the ideas of Grimké and Fuller are combined, the result is a roughly hewn, but nonetheless complete, feminist ideology. Grimké offered a concise, analytical survey of woman's status in society and recommended ways to improve it. Fuller explained this status and justified its alteration in philosophical terms. The arguments both ideologists made not only established a new ideology of feminism, but also resulted in one of the most enduring ideologies of the modern world. As we shall see, the analyses contributed by Grimké and Fuller, and especially the conclusions they reached, are as valid today as they were over a century ago.

AN ABOLITIONIST'S CASE FOR FEMINISM

Sarah Grimké's criticisms of woman's status in society, upon initial examination, appear very similar to those of Wollstonecraft and the socialist feminists. Grimké viewed man as a tyrant who, after enslaving and debasing woman for centuries, claimed she was inferior. Grimké criticized Wollstonecraft's middle-class woman for allowing herself to be a plaything for man whose only goal in life was an advantageous marriage. She also reiterated Wright's intense criticisms of woman's lack of political, civil, and legal rights, especially the lack of rights inherent in a democratic society—the rights of property and economic freedom. But while she made these standard feminist arguments, Grimké's economic, political, and religious analyses were both more complex and more fully developed. She made several contributions to the development of feminist ideology, contributions that are often attributed to twentieth-century feminism.

Grimké, for example, clearly explicated the meaning of political, legal, economic, and social equality for woman. She defined economic equality as equal pay for equal work. She distinguished for the first time in feminist thought the differences between legal and political equality. In her recommendations for change she advocated a broader based program of change for woman, including representation in government, the right of contract, and legal participation on juries. In brief, Grimké advocated complete equality for woman based on her human rights. She negated differentiations in society based on sex and in her analysis defined the meaning of "sexism." This expansion of feminism to include specific recommendations for equality and an emphasis on woman's human and moral rights to equality evolved from Grimké's Abolitionist perspective. She adopted the democratic values and goals of the American Revolution and applied them to woman, just as the Abolitionists applied them to the American Negro slaves. She, like other Abolitionists, prescribed complete legal, political, economic, and social equality. Grimké herself recognized that her concern for woman's status emanated from her investigation into the status and rights of slaves.

> The investigation of the rights of the slave has led me to a better understanding of my own. I have found the Anti-Slavery cause to be the high school of morals in our land—the school in which *human rights* are more fully investigated, and better understood and taught, than in any other. . . . Human beings have *rights*, because they are *moral* beings.[1]

In her discussion of woman's enslaved condition in society, Grimké relied upon this perspective in analyzing woman. She compared woman's role in society with that of the Negro slaves. "I shall not find it difficult to show, that in all ages and countries, not even excepting enlightened republican America, woman has more or less been made a means to promote the welfare of man, without due regard to her own happiness."[2] Woman, then, had no individual "ends" in society. She was only a means for man's goals.

One group of women ignored by earlier feminists particularly concerned Grimké: the female slaves in America. Men were most tyrannical in their oppressive dehumanization of female slaves. Grimké's feminist analysis thus expanded the scope of feminism to include all women in society, not merely the middle class, as in Wollstonecraft, or the working and middle classes, as in Wright and Tristan. All women, free and enslaved, should be equal to free men. Grimké's concern for female slaves is particularly interesting because Wright, who was also an Abolitionist and founded the Negro Nashoba community, ignored it.

On the controversial issue of innate female inferiority and equality, Grimké again took a more positive and stronger position than did Wollstonecraft, Wright, or Tristan. For Grimké, woman was unequivocably man's moral and intellectual equal.

> If they mean to intimate, that mental or moral weakness belongs to woman, more than to man, I utterly disclaim the charge. Our powers of mind have been crushed, as far as man could do it, our sense of morality has been impaired by his interpretation of our duties; but no where does God say that he made any distinction between us as moral and intelligent beings.[3]

These conclusions contained none of Wollstonecraft's doubts; nor were they couched in the apologetic arguments of Wollstonecraft and Wright that unless woman became more of an intellectual and moral equal to man the human race would not progress. Grimké's justification for intellectual equality was expressed simply. "Intellect is not sexed."[4] Grimké extended these arguments for innate female equality when she also contended that given the necessary physical exercise and training, "women are capable of acquiring as great physical power as men."[5]

In her evaluation of woman's status in society, Grimké continued to take stronger positions favoring female equality than any of her predecessors. While Frances Wright was concerned with the political rights of woman and how to achieve them, Sarah Grimké was the first feminist to differentiate between political and legal rights. Political rights for Grimké were those inherent in a democratic society. First, woman was taxed without representation. "And this taxation, be it remembered, was the cause of our Revolutionary war . . . yet the daughters of New England, as well as of all the other States of this free Republic, are suffering a similar injustice."[6] Second, woman was tried under laws she had no role in making and convicted by juries whose members were not her peers.[7] Grimké's analysis of woman's political stature thus exceeded in specificity and scope that of the earlier feminists by advocating female equality in both the framing and execution of the laws. Such extensive political equality obviously necessitated female representation in the criminal justice system as well as female enfranchisement, steps which were not taken until the next century. In fact, it was not until the 1960s that the Supreme Court required the representation of Negroes and women on juries when the defendant was Negro or female.

Grimké's analysis of woman's economic status was similarly more sophisticated than that of earlier feminists. Her criticisms were not limited to woman's lack of occupational and professional equality, as were Wright's and Tristan's, but also included denunciation of the practice of paying women less for their work than men were paid for the same job, that is, the contemporary equal pay for equal work issue.[8] This economic inequality, Grimké concluded, enslaved both men and women.

> Many women are now supported, in idleness and extravagance, by the industry of their husbands, fathers, or brothers, who are compelled to toil out their existence, at the counting house, or in the printing office, or some other laborious occupation, while the wife and daughters and sisters take no part in the support of the family, and appear to think that their sole business is to spend the hard bought earnings of their male friends. I deeply regret such a state of things, because I believe that if women felt their responsibility, for the support of themselves or their families it would add strength and dignity to their characters, and teach them more true sympathy for their husbands, than is now generally manifested—a sympathy which would be exhibited by actions as well as words.[9]

This equalization of status would benefit men as well as women.

Probably Grimké's most pronounced deviation from earlier feminist ideologists, however, was her analysis and attempt to deal with religion's role in subjugating woman. The religious issue was one with which all earlier feminists had dealt, but one whose resolution they skirted. Wollstonecraft and Tristan, for example, recognized religion's detrimental effects on woman but sought to expand woman's sphere of knowledge beyond the religious. Wright advocated abolishing religion, an unrealistic proposition. Grimké, in contrast, attempted to disprove religion's arguments and justifications for female inferiority.

Recognizing the importance of religion for the human psyche and social existence, Grimké attempted to demonstrate that religion was supportive of female equality and that it was only the dogma and priesthoods of the existing misinformed religions that proclaimed woman's inferiority. In form, Grimké's arguments were an appeal to both the literal and inherent meanings of the scriptures. In her analysis, she rejected the King James version of the Bible, the version that was used by American anti-feminists, for an earlier Catholic version. Her rationale for doing so was that the King James version and other Protestant versions were revised late in the history of Christianity. The King James Bible thus reflected later Christian thought that incorporated the anti-feminist ideas of Saint Augustine and Reformation thinkers.

Grimké based her assertion that the scriptures supported female equality by focusing on accounts of the creation in the Book of Genesis. Unlike the King James Bible, Catholic bibles do not contain the description of woman as coming from "Adam's rib." Rather, man and woman were equal at their creation, both formed in God's image. "Dominion was given to both over every other creature, but not over each other. Created in perfect equality, they were expected to exercise the viceregence intrusted to them by their Maker, in harmony and love."[10]

Extending her analysis of the scriptures, Grimké next focused on the "fall" of Adam and Eve in the Garden of Eden. Eve's participation in the fall from grace was used by the clergy to prove that woman was an evil being, or at least immoral, who was therefore inherently man's inferior. In particular, the arguments that woman was a creature of passion and emotion lacking in reason were based on the Biblical story of the fall. Grimké argued, on the contrary, that woman was no more responsible for the fall from God's grace than was man. "There was as much weakness exhibited by Adam as by Eve. They both fell from innocence, and consequently from happiness, but not from equality."[11]

The superior status of man for Grimké thus was not founded in scripture or theology. Men and women were equal, even if they were equally guilty, before God. In fact, Grimké contended, man may have been more a fallen creature than woman. Man's passions for power and superiority exemplified his corrupt nature.[12]

Grimké's final defense of female equality against religious opposition was a very logical one. Basically, if woman really was as inferior as man portrayed her to be and if she recognized man's superiority, then woman would be guilty of idolatry, thus breaking the first of God's commandments. Because of her human status, woman logically could not be innately inferior to man. If God had created her as an inferior being, she could not be bound to the commandments in the same way and degree as man. And if she was exempt from God's commandments, then woman could not share guilt with man for the fall from grace. Yet, Grimké noted, woman did share man's punishment and guilt.[13]

Whether or not Grimké successfully refuted and disproved clerical arguments for female inferiority is not really an issue in this analysis. What is important is that she recognized the futility of advocating the abolition of religion and the ineffectiveness of secular education as a means for circumventing religious dogma. Grimké realized that religion in her time was an important and powerful social force with unrivaled influence on the population. The only effective means for counteracting religion's anti-feminist stance was to undermine the efficacy of this dogma by rational debate, analysis, and discourse. Any actions more radical than this would be rejected without thought or discussion. Anything less radical would be ineffective in even raising doubts about religion's bias against women. For this reason, Grimké's handling of the religious problem was more realistic than earlier feminist analyses.

Grimké's most significant and unique contribution to the development of feminist ideology in her analysis of woman's status in society was her identification of the phenomenon of "sexism." She criticized the whole mode of thought that differentiated between male and female, much as Stokely Carmichael in *Black Power* defined racism as racial differentiation. Men and women for Grimké were human, nothing more or less.

> We approach each other, and mingle with each other, under the constant pressure of a feeling that we are of different sexes; and, instead of regarding each other only in the light of immortal creatures, the mind is fettered by the idea which is early and industriously infused into it, that we must never forget the distinction between male and female. Hence our intercourse, instead of being elevated and refined, is generally calculated to excite and keep alive the lowest propensities of our nature. Nothing, I believe, has tended more to destroy the true dignity of woman, than the fact that she is approached by man in the character of a female. The idea that she is sought as an intelligent and heaven-born creature, whose society will refine and elevate her companion, and that she will receive the same blessings she confers, is rarely held up to her view. On the contrary, man almost always addresses himself to the weakness of woman.[14]

Grimké's analysis of woman's status in society was thus more comprehensive than any of the earlier feminist ideologists. She was critical not only of tangible economic, political, legal, educational, and religious discrimination against women, but also discriminatory perspectives, modes of thought, and value orientations that distorted perceptions of the true roles and nature of woman. Given such comprehensive criticisms of woman in society, curiosity about Grimké's prescriptions naturally arises. Simply put, Grimké believed woman should be equal to man. This equality should encompass all aspects of life and exclude sexual differentiation. "Woman must feel that she is the equal, and is designed to be the fellow laborer of her brother, or she will be studying to find out the imaginary line which separates the sexes, and divides the duties of men and women into two distinct classes."[15]

Grimké's programs for achieving female equality were as simple as her prescription of equality. She developed no complicated educational systems, no total restructuring of society along socialist lines, or other complex, long-range means. For Grimké, woman should achieve her own equality by utilizing whatever freedom she possessed to her full advantage. Woman should assert herself on behalf of her own equality. Woman's equality was woman's struggle, and male educators or legislators were not to be relied upon.

> One of the duties which devolve upon women in the present interesting crisis, is to prepare themselves for more extensive usefulness, by making use of those religious and literary privileges and advantages that are within their reach, if they will only stretch out their hands and possess them. By doing this, they will become better acquainted with their rights as moral beings, and with their responsibilities growing out of those rights: they will regard themselves, as they really are, FREE AGENTS, immortal beings.[16]

While this program of self-help could be criticized today on the grounds that woman would first need to acquire a desire for total equality, which she would not necessarily possess, it was quite valid for Grimké's era. During Grimké's life, women were asserting themselves for the first time in Western history, and there was no reason to believe that the process would be reversed. It also would have been naive to believe that male legislators would institute female equality or even the right to vote because men were responsible for keeping women subjugated.

For Grimké's time, then, her strategy—woman achieving her own equality by asserting herself—seemed much more promising than the programs of Wollstonecraft's rational education and the socialist feminists' socialist society. In fact, history has thus far proved Grimké's strategy the best. The right to vote was achieved by women after decades of radical activity and the changing social climate that it engendered. Equal employment and educational opportunities were achieved because women sought them and pushed for them, not because benevolent male legislators determined that they were necessary for a truly democratic state. Finally, the difficulty in getting the Equal Rights Amendment, a legislated dictum, ratified because of public opposition demonstrates that legislation alone cannot achieve equality.

Grimké's feminist writings, in retrospect, reveal the depth of her understanding of woman's societal oppression. She advocated female equality, such as equal representation on juries and equal pay for equal work, with a specificity uncommon with the earlier feminists. She attempted to refute intellectual arguments supporting woman's subjugation rather than propose means for circumventing those arguments. In short, Grimké's contributions to the development of feminist ideology were significant because she delineated both an extensive analysis of woman's inferior status in society and prescriptions for equalizing woman's role. Her ideology, however, like earlier feminist ideologies, failed to take into account one important component of any theory. She failed to define the object of her analysis—woman. Grimké, while describing how society oppressed woman, never defined how this oppression affected woman as a thinking being, and what woman could become without it. This task was left to Margaret Fuller.

THE PHILOSOPHICAL BASES OF FEMINIST IDEOLOGY

Margaret Fuller was a vital member of the American Transcendentalist circle consisting of Ralph Waldo Emerson, Henry David Thoreau, W.A. Channing, and others. Many historians, in fact, conclude that Fuller was one of the four leading Transcendentalists of her time.[17] Editor of *The Dial* (a Transcendentalist journal) before Emerson, she was a life-long student of philosophy with a special interest in Greek philosophy and mythology and German philosophy, particularly Goethe.

Fuller's renowned treatise on woman, *Woman in the Nineteenth Century*, was a conscious and conscientious attempt to apply the philosophical tenets of Transcendentalism to woman. The scope and depth of this comprehensive, cogent, and critical appraisal of the status of American women in the nineteenth century was far superior to any earlier feminist writings. Indeed, if any feminist treatise of the nineteenth century warrants consideration as feminist ideology in and of itself, that work would be *Woman in the Nineteenth Century*.

In her analysis of woman in the nineteenth century, Fuller incorporated what she considered the most valid facets of earlier feminist writings while rejecting others as detrimental to the progress of woman. For example, like all earlier feminists, Fuller criticized woman's coquetry and childish vanity, asserting that she "does not look beyond the pleasure of making herself felt at the moment."[18] Man was responsible for this ignorant state. "He educated Woman more as a servant than a daughter, and found himself a king without a queen. The children of this unequal union showed unequal natures."[19]

Like the socialist feminists, Fuller also was concerned with the degree of influence that the priesthood exerted over the minds of women. Fuller, however, did not perceive the priesthood as a malevolent force as did the socialists. The priesthood rather was able to impose its views upon woman simply because woman's intellect had not developed sufficiently to counteract its influence. Hence, Fuller advocated not the abolition of religion but the development of woman. "Women are, indeed, the easy victims both of priestcraft and self-delusion; but this would not be, if the intellect was developed in proportion to the other powers. They would then have a regulator, and be more in equipoise."[20]

A final point of similarity between Fuller and the earlier feminist ideologists was her discussion of the physical inferiority of woman. Fuller believed with Grimké that woman could become as physically powerful as man. Although she was not concerned with proving woman's physical equality for its own sake, Fuller believed woman's lack of physical development should not be utilized as a reason for keeping her out of the political sphere. "Those who think the physical circumstances of Woman would make a part in the affairs of government unsuitable, are by no means those who think it impossible for negresses to endure field-work."[21]

At this point, Fuller took leave of the earlier feminists. She was openly critical of some earlier feminist analyses, especially their prescriptions, and rejected them as superficial solutions to the complex problem of female inequality. While earlier feminists were concerned either with the ramifications of woman's inferior status on woman and society or the societal factors that rendered her inferior, Fuller was more concerned with woman herself. She emphasized the necessity of the individual development of each woman, not the improvement of society and making woman a better social actor.

Because of her orientation toward the individual development of woman, Fuller was particularly critical of the socialist feminists, who made the progress of woman merely one facet of the progress of society as a whole toward a socialist structure. This, she said, restricted the ability of socialist prescriptions to equalize woman's status. Indeed, the nature of socialist society itself inhibited individual development. "Why bind oneself to a central or any doctrine? How much nobler stands a man entirely unpledged, unbound! Association may be the great experiment of the age, still it is only an experiment."[22] The binding of the human character to one doctrine made man (and woman) a creature of society, rather than society a creature of man.[23] As a creature of society, man's individuality and genius would be stifled. "If any individual live too much in relations, so that he becomes a stranger to the resources of his own nature, he falls, after a while, into a distraction or imbecility."[24] In Fuller's opinion, therefore, the socialist feminists' prescriptions and programs for improving the status of woman by restructuring society along socialist lines were both ineffective and detrimental to the individual development of woman. Woman would be as stifled and controlled in a socialist society as she was under male domination.

Fuller was also very critical of the assumption made by Wollstonecraft and Tristan that if woman were more developed intellectually and emotionally she would be a better wife and mother. The concern of the early feminists that woman should be more equal so that she could contribute to the progress of the race for Fuller was seeking the right ends for the wrong reasons. Woman should achieve equality for its own sake. The reason for female equality must be to develop the capabilities of the individual woman. Fuller concluded that "the intellect, no more than the sense of hearing, is to be cultivated merely that Woman may be a more valuable companion to Man, but because the Power who gave a power, by its mere existence signifies that it must be brought out toward perfection."[25] In fact, Fuller argued, woman should not necessarily be programmed to be wives and mothers at all. Woman should enter into marriage only after careful and intensive consideration by a well-developed intellect free from pressures of society and family.

Fuller's rejection of several important prescriptions and goals of earlier feminists induced her to develop unique criticisms of woman's status in society and prescriptions for changing this status. She emphasized the importance of woman achieving freedom as an individual and as an intellect. Freedom was a democratic right, one which had been denied woman throughout history in the Western democracies. This freedom for woman to participate in democratic society and develop her intellectual potential through social inter-course was woman's right both because she possessed a human soul and because she belonged to a democratic society.

> Yet, then and only then will mankind be ripe for this, when inward and outward freedom for Woman as much as for Man shall be acknowledged as a *right*, not yielded as a concession. As the friend of the negro assumes that one man cannot by right hold another in bondage, so should the friend of Woman assume that Man cannot by right lay even well-meant restrictions on Woman.[26]

Unlike the earlier feminists who were preoccupied with woman's freedom in society and politics, Fuller extended her criticisms of woman's freedom beyond these external freedoms. Of primary importance for Fuller was that woman should develop internal freedom, not merely intellectual freedom (the ability to be rational that preoccupied Wollstonecraft), nor moral and spiritual freedom from the priesthood (which particularly concerned Wright and Tristan). Fuller's internal freedom encompassed all aspects of human existence.

> It is not the transient breath of poetic incense that women want; each can receive that from a lover. It is not life-long sway; it needs but to become a coquette, a shrew, or a good cook, to be sure of that. It is not money, nor notoriety, nor the badges of authority which men have appropriated themselves. If demands, made in their behalf, lay stress on any of these particulars, those who make them have not searched deeply into the need. The want is for that which at once includes these and precludes them; which would not be forbidden power, lest there be temptation to steal and misuse it; which would not have the mind perverted by flattery from a worthiness of esteem; it is for that which is the birthright of every being capable of re-

ceiving it—the freedom, the religious, the intellectual freedom of the universe to use its means, to learn its secrets, as far as Nature has enabled them, with God alone for their guide and their judge. Ye cannot believe it, men; but the only reason why women never assume what is more appropriate to you, is because you prevent them from finding out what is fit for themselves. Were they free, were they wise fully to develop the strength and beauty of Woman; they would never wish to be men, or manlike.[27]

Fuller thus prescribed that woman should have the freedom to develop the essence of her human character and potential. This metaphysical analysis of woman's needs was borrowed from Goethe. In essence, Fuller expanded and to some extent individualized from her female perspective Goethe's concept of self-culture, which may also be defined as self-realization. Fuller herself credited Goethe for providing a basis for her description of internal freedom. "The aim of Goethe is satisfactory to me. He aims at a pure self-subsistence, and a free development of any powers with which they may be gifted by nature as much for them as for men."[28]

Fuller at base believed that if woman developed internal freedom and realized her potential as a human, she would soon discover that she was a unique being. In this definition of woman's uniqueness, Fuller made her most significant contribution to the development of feminist ideology. She defined a quality in woman, a part of the female being and psyche, not found in man—a quality which rendered woman man's superior in some ways. This unique quality Fuller named "femality."

Femality was the "electrical" and "magnetic" element in woman. It was the force that enabled her intuitive and perceptive powers to be more intense and quick-acting than man's. Woman possessed "unimpeded clearness of the intuitive powers,"[29] which resulted in her intuitions being more rapid and correct than those of man. "She excels not so easily in classification, or recreation, as in an instinctive seizure of causes, and a simple breathing out of what she receives, that has the singleness of life, rather than the selecting and energizing of art."[30]

Fuller, however, did not terminate her analysis of woman's need for self-development with her definition of woman's uniqueness.

She concluded instead that if woman possessed a unique quality then woman should seek her own identity and not continue to emulate man. Man was too bound by the traditions and habits of society that evolved under his tutelage. Woman had never created her own bonds because she lacked freedom. Since she was inherently different from man, she could be bound to neither him nor to his society. Woman, for Fuller, was society's hope for the future. Woman's future role in society was to arouse the consciousness of all humanity.[31]

In this discussion of femality and woman's special capacity for freeing (raising the consciousness of) the human race, Fuller most significantly deviated from her predecessors. Fuller extended woman's role in society beyond that of being an educated helpmate of man to possessing equal rights and status with man in society. While woman should seek equal rights with man based on her human status, she should not limit her goals to mere de facto or even de jure equality. Woman should assume, on the contrary, her proper role in society as a planner and prophet of the future. Only through woman's innate femality could the oppressive habits and traditions of society be eliminated. Only through woman's role in raising human consciousness, not through male legislators or socialist societies, was significant social change possible.

Given Fuller's analysis of woman as a unique being in some ways superior to man and better suited to improving society than he, it is understandable that Fuller's prescriptions for improving woman's status in society should significantly differ from those of earlier feminists. Only Grimké's conclusion that woman must better herself approximated Fuller's prescriptions and programs, and then for very different reasons.

Fuller's initial prescription for woman's future status in society was that woman should be a complete being. In developing her femality and obtaining equal rights, woman should attain perfection in being, or a complete life. She should develop her faculties to the highest degree and cultivate her essence as a female human being. Crucial to this development was woman's total independence from man. Independence of the sexes was not an end in itself for Fuller, as she did not assert that either sex would be able to exist without the other, but it was a needed means for woman to develop her potential. Since man was bound by traditional notions of the correct roles and status for woman, he inhibited woman's self-realization. "I have urged on Woman independence from Man, not that I do not think the sexes mutually needed by one another, but because in Woman this fact has led to an excessive devotion, which has cooled love, degraded marriage, and prevented either sex from being what it should be to itself or the other."[32]

Woman's independence from man and unique femality necessitated for Fuller a unique education and economic equality. Fuller was the first feminist ideologist to propose that woman not be given the same education as man. She believed that the education men received was insufficient to develop woman's character.[33] Yet, while Fuller realized that a new system of education was needed to develop the newly identified femality of woman, her proposal for this new system was inadequate. She failed to describe the system of education that she believed. necessary, including modes and content of instruction. This failure to delineate a fundamental part of her prescription for woman's future weakened Fuller's analysis.

A similar oversight or weakness may be found in her advocacy of equal employment opportunities for woman. While she claimed for woman, "let them be sea-captains if you will,"[34] she provided no guidance for how woman was to acquire the expertise necessary to assume the variety of occupations open to men. If traditional education was insufficient for woman, then what should replace it?

Therefore, while Fuller in general terms advocated a special system of education for woman and equal employment opportunities, she offered no concrete guidelines for achieving either of these goals. Woman was to achieve her own potential by acting on her own behalf—the same strategy that Grimké delineated for woman's attainment of equality in society. For both Grimké and Fuller, man's role in the equalization of woman's status should be passive, at the least not interfering and at the most eliminating the "arbitrary barriers" they imposed on women. Man's reliance upon traditional authority rendered him unable to create an equal place in society for woman.

Fuller's strategy of self-help, however, actually was the only strategy that she could have developed given her analysis of woman's essence and nature. If woman possessed unique qualities, then man would be unqualified to structure woman's freedom. As Fuller concluded when discussing a special system of education for woman, woman must define her own needs and develop the means for fulfilling them. Man could only be her helpmate. "I believe that, at present, women are the best helpers of one another. Let them think; let them act; till they know what they need."[35]

Margaret Fuller, in conclusion, offered a more unique analysis of woman's status in society and future goals than the earlier feminists. While her prescriptions and programs for woman may have been too general to provide practical guidelines on how to achieve a new societal status, Fuller still developed the most complex and sophisticated feminist ideology of her era. Fuller was the first feminist to extend her analysis beyond woman's societal role. The earlier feminists were concerned about woman's intellectual and moral development, a concern based on the contributions that more equal women could make to the development of society and the human race. Fuller's ideology, in contrast, focused on woman herself. Her single goal was improving woman's human condition. Fuller could easily be criticized for this goal of individual rather than societal improvement. Her ideology could easily be labelled by some to be individualistic if not narcissistic, and perhaps even detrimental to society as a whole. Contemporary opponents of the women's movement might find in Fuller an example of extremism. They could claim that Fuller advocated an Amazonian type of society in her conclusion that woman's unique quality of femality made her better equipped to innovate societal change.

Yet Fuller's feminist ideology was neither extremist nor narcissistic, nor even individualistic. It was rather an attempt to come to terms with an issue not raised by earlier feminists—what is "woman"? All of Fuller's predecessors concluded that woman had not reached her potential. Her intellectual, moral, and emotional development was stymied. They delineated a variety of methods to implement a societal environment conducive to woman's development. But none of them first considered the prerequisite issues of woman's nature and how change could be structured before woman's real nature was defined. In other words, the early feminists defined the means of improving woman's condition without first defining the condition woman was capable of attaining, perhaps because they assumed woman was a potential man. While Fuller's ideology was lacking in means, she at least recognized the importance of first uncovering woman's nature and defining her potential.

Fuller's significance as a feminist ideologist lies in this preoccupation with analyzing woman's human condition. While other feminists investigated and analyzed woman as an oppressed and subjugated creature, Fuller analyzed woman as a unique being. In this identification of woman's nature, or at least an attempt to do so, Fuller constructed the philosophical bases of feminist ideology.

Fuller's focus on the nature of woman is understandable in light of her philosophical proclivities. Like the Greek and German philosophers she emulated, Fuller was committed primarily to the discovery of the individual's quality of being and nature of existence. This concern was the result of her Transcendentalist perspective.

Contemporary historians and theorists, in fact, long have acknowledged the impact of Fuller's Transcendentalism on *Woman in the Nineteenth Century*. Perry Miller observed, for instance,

> It is a pioneer work for the "feminist" movement in America. . . . Just as the Transcendental metaphysic inevitably supplied bases for a new critique of the social structure, so it could not avoid posing the problem of the relation between the sexes in new terms, arguing for sexual equality. Not only could man become Man thinking by walking in the open air, but so also, at least theoretically, could woman.[36]

Fuller thus came to be a feminist ideologist because she was the Transcendentalist most concerned with woman.

Fuller's Transcendental philosophy and, consequently, her feminist ideology can best be evaluated by comparing them to the philosophy of Ralph Waldo Emerson. He more than anyone else established the scope and content of American Transcendentalism. Emerson's essay, "The Transcendentalist," like treatises of other Transcendentalists, revealed Transcendentalism's narrow focus on the human condition. While the Transcendentalists described a future utopian society built upon their recommendations, only peripherally did they discuss man's relationship to society. Similarly, when they developed prescriptions and programs for changing society, they focused more on developing the ideal, or transcendent, individual and only fantasized about a transcendental society.

For Emerson, Transcendentalism was above all idealism. Its primary goal was human development and fulfillment, not in relation to societal structures, but the development of the mind and true spiritual nature of man. In Emerson's words, "The height, the deity of man is to be self-sustained, to need no gift, no foreign force."[37] The Transcendentalists thus rejected the utopian socialist notion of man as the product of his environment. They asserted that, while the immanent (non-transcendent) individual could be controlled by circumstances because he lacked the spiritual power to control his own mind, the individual who achieved transcendence created his own circumstances.

In defining the transcendental personality, Emerson offered the following description.

> He believes in miracles, in the perpetual openness of the human mind to new influx of light and power; he believes in inspiration, and in ecstasy. He wishes that the spiritual principle should be suffered to demonstrate itself to the end, in all possible applications to the state of man, without the admission of anything spiritual; that is, anything positive, dogmatic, personal. Thus, the spiritual measure of inspiration is the depth of the thought, and never, who said it? And so he resists all attempts to palm other rules and measures on the spirit than its own.[38]

A transcendent individual was thus an individual who possessed a class of ideas (or form) which did not emanate from sensory experience but through which experience was acquired. The ideal transcendentalist utilized intuition as the motivating force in life. Intuitions were respected and given control over life's sensory experiences.

Transcendentalism as a philosophy not only defined the transcendent individual as moral and intuitive but also provided guidelines for aiding the individual in achieving a state of transcendence. Most importantly, the individual seeking transcendence recognized God's immanence and the unity of the world in God. He knew that the soul of each individual is identical to the soul of the world and of nature. Through the goodness of the natural world, the individual's soul could become part of the spirit and being of God. In sum, the transcendent individual continuously attempted to expand the potential elements of his being until he approximated the spirit of God. "Intuition—that is the method of the transcendentalist philosophy; no truth worth the knowing is susceptible of logical demonstration."[39] Intuition was the Transcendentalists' means of acquiring knowledge.

From this theory, Emerson and other theorists of Transcendentalism like Channing, Thoreau, and Alcott expanded the philosophy to include practical guidelines for the individual living in the sensational (non-transcendent) world. They indicated patterns of action for the individual to guide the development of his potential and intuition in a world ruled by sensory experience. Primarily, the Transcendentalists advocated a doctrine of self-reliance and individualism. Each individual should rely on his own intuition—not experience, reason, or societal or governmental laws—for controlling his life. Henry David Thoreau's essay "Civil Disobedience" was the most famous statement of this theory of the individual's responsibility for his own life.

Beyond this, in their prescriptions for improving society, the Transcendentalists projected the potential impact of their philosophy on what they considered the vital components of society—physics, politics, ethics, and religion. They constructed a utopian prescription for a transcendent society but without identifying any courses of action for achieving their utopia. They instead directed their attention to implementing Transcendentalist values by changing the individual.[40]

Of all the leading Transcendentalists, Margaret Fuller was the most practically oriented. Her theory was less constrained by the spiritual nature of Transcendentalism. She was, as James Freeman Clarke suggested, a "realist,"[41] and so she constructed more comprehensive analyses of the negative influence that existing societal structures had on the individual than the other Transcendentalists. She wrote, "In a word, the tendency of circumstances has been to make our people superficial, irreverent, and more anxious to get a living than to live mentally and morally."[42]

Despite her emphasis on the effect of circumstances on the immanent (as contrasted with the transcendent) individual, Fuller accepted and used all major components of Transcendentalism. Both her general works on Transcendentalism and her analysis in

Woman in the Nineteenth Century reflected her Transcendentalist orientation. She acknowledged the primary importance of human development and fulfillment, "For human beings are not so constituted that they can live without expansion. If they do not get it in one way, they must in another, or perish."[43] Like other Transcendentalists, she believed both in the power of inspiration and in the importance of acquiring knowledge through intuition instead of sensory experience. She contended that the human soul was identical to the souls of God and the world and that the individual must become self-reliant and a complete individual. Even in her criticisms of society and recommendations for changing it, Fuller approximated the beliefs of the other Transcendentalists, arguing, like Emerson, that moral and physical laws were identical, that religions should be united, and that the individual should disregard authority and tradition. These Transcendentalist beliefs were the basis of her analysis of woman in the nineteenth century.

In *Woman in the Nineteenth Century*, Fuller initially focused on the issue of woman's development and fulfillment. She applied the Transcendentalist goal of the transcendent individual—the individual who developed his mind and met his potential—to woman in a very cogent analysis. First, Fuller asserted that woman possessed the right of self-fulfillment just as man did, based on her human nature. Woman deserved self-fulfillment and equality because she was part of the human community, not because she should be a better wife and mother, as Wollstonecraft and the earlier feminists had argued.

Second, Fuller applied the Transcendentalist goal of the intuitive individual to woman. Fuller asserted that woman was more capable than man of assuming a state of transcendence because her femality, woman's special intuitive nature, rendered her superior to man. This identification of a special quality in woman's character, and in general her concern with defining woman's character, was part of her contribution to the development of feminist ideology. While earlier ideologists concerned themselves with woman's relationship to society and man and developed prescriptions and strategies for improving those relationships, Fuller established analyzing woman herself as a prerequisite for analyzing woman's relationship to society. Without knowing woman's nature, improving that nature and human condition by changing society was impossible.

Fuller's Transcendentalist perspective also led her to claim that woman was superior to man. She constructed the following argument. For the Transcendentalists, the extent of an individual's intuitive powers was the primary criterion for evaluating his or her transcendence or ideal state. If woman innately possessed greater intuitive powers than man, then woman must be superior to man. From this assertion, several prescriptions for improving woman and society necessarily followed. First, woman could not be controlled by man. Second, man could not educate woman because she possessed greater potential for transcendence and because man kept woman in a state of immanence. Third, since woman retained the potential for developing more intuitive powers than man, woman must be the social planner and prophet of the future. Only woman with her higher intuitive powers could overcome the societal traditions and authority man had created, the traditions and authority that the other Transcendentalists identified as particularly stifling to the development of transcendence.

In addition to her application of the Transcendentalist goals of human self-fulfillment and intuition in woman, Fuller also applied the concept of a human soul as identical to God's and the importance of self-reliance to woman's condition. She contended that woman, like man, possessed a soul, and that woman's soul was not derivative of man's, but separate and equal. "Women are in themselves possessors of and possessed by immortal souls."[44] Because woman's soul was identical to God's, man could not control woman. Woman's soul guaranteed her human rights to self-fulfillment and self-reliance. Woman had the right and responsibility to develop her own potential.

When discussing woman's right to self-reliance, however, Fuller developed her strongest arguments for woman's improvement and equality. The combination of woman's superior intuitive powers and soul provided the right to self-determination and self-reliance. Woman should seek her own identity and not rely upon man to define either her social roles as wife and mother (Fuller believed that woman should seriously think about becoming either), her life-style, character, or development as a human being. "I have urged on Woman independence of Man, not that I think the sexes mutually exclusive, but because in Woman this fact has led to excessive devotion, which has cooled love, degraded marriage, and prevented either sex from being what it should be to itself or the other."[45] "It is not Woman, but the law of right, the law of growth, that speaks in us, and demands the perfection of each being in its kind—apple as apple, woman as woman."[46]

Fuller thus applied the important tenets of Transcendentalism to woman's human condition. From this application, Fuller constructed new analyses of woman and new prescriptions for changing woman's status. Her analyses of woman deviated significantly from the earlier feminist ideologists. She was the first ideologist to demonstrate concern for woman as woman. By posing the question What is woman? she identified the innate characteristics of woman's character. Woman was intuitive and, consequently, superior. Then drawing upon her definition of woman's character, Fuller constructed prescriptions and programs for woman's self-improvement and the improvement of woman's relationship to society. Woman must help herself. She must control society because of her greater potential for inspiration and intuition. These contributions by Fuller to the development of feminist ideology were the philosophical bases of both nineteenth- and twentieth-century feminist ideology. These philosophical bases developed from Fuller's Transcendentalist perspective.

NOTES

1. Sarah Grimké, *Letters on the Equality of the Sexes, and the Condition of Woman, Addressed to Mary S. Parker, President of the Boston Female Anti-Slavery Society* (Boston: Isaac Knapp, 1838), p. 114.

2. Ibid., p. 12.

3. Ibid., p. 14.

4. Ibid., p. 33.

5. Ibid., p. 29.

6. Ibid., pp. 80-81.

7. Ibid., p. 83.

8. Ibid., p. 50.

9. Ibid., pp. 54-55.

10. Ibid., pp. 4-5.

11. Ibid., pp. 6-7.

12. Ibid., p. 94.

13. Ibid., p. 115.

14. Ibid., pp. 22-23.

15. Ibid., p. 116.

16. Ibid., pp. 121-22.

17. For example, Harold Clarke Goddard, *Studies in New England Transcendentalism* (New York: Hillary House, 1960), p. 115; Perry Miller, ed., *The Transcendentalists: An Anthology* (Cambridge: Harvard University Press, 1950), p. 332; and Walter L. Leighton, *French Philosophers and New England Transcendentalism* (New York: Greenwood Press, 1968), p. 61.

18. Margaret Fuller Ossoli, *Woman in the Nineteenth Century, and Kindred Papers Relating to the Sphere, Condition, and Duties of Woman,* ed. Arthur B. Fuller (Boston: Brown, Taggard and Chase, 1860), p. 62.

19. Ibid., p. 49.

20. Ibid., p. 171.

21. Ibid., p. 105.

22. Ibid., p. 35.

23. Margaret Fuller, quoted in R.W. Emerson et al., *Memoirs of Margaret Fuller Ossoli,* 2 vols. (Boston: Brown, Taggard and Chase, 1860), II: 75.

24. Ibid., II: 28.

25. Fuller, *Woman*, p. 119.

26. Ibid., pp. 70-71.

27. Ibid., p. 37.

28. Ibid., p. 125.

29. Ibid., p. 128.

30. Ibid., p. 115.

31. Ibid., pp. 119-20.

32. Ibid., p. 175.

33. Ibid., pp. 94-95.

34. Ibid., p. 174.

35. Ibid., p. 172.

36. Miller, *Transcendentalists*, p. 457.

37. Ralph Waldo Emerson, "The Transcendentalist," in *The Transcendentalist Revolt Against Materialism,* ed. George F. Whicher (Boston: D.C. Heath and Company, 1949), p. 20.

38. Ibid.

39. Goddard, *Studies in Transcendentalism*, p. 5.

40. Theodore Parker, in Whicher, *Transcendentalist Revolt*, p. 82.

41. James Freeman Clarke, in R. W. Emerson et al., *Memoirs*, I: 113.

42. Fuller, quoted in Ibid., II: 27.

43. Fuller, *Woman*, p. 36.

44. Ibid., p. 56.

45. Ibid., p. 175,

46. Ibid., p. 177.

Feminist Ideology: The Middle Years, 1845-1945

AFTER THE MID-1840S AND the publication of works on woman by Grimké and Fuller, innovation in the development of feminist ideology ceased. By 1850 the "women's movement" was a well-publicized force in American and British social and political spheres. Women's Rights Conventions were held in Ohio and Massachusetts in which women predominated as speakers and participants. Women began making demands on the political system for the right of suffrage. While some economic and social demands were made on behalf of women, the focus of women's activism quickly became the right to vote. It is therefore understandable that the content of feminist analyses of woman's status in society gradually became restricted to the right to vote and the advantages of suffrage for women. But while focusing on this one issue increased the chances of achieving female suffrage, the increasing narrowness of women's vision hindered the further development and sophistication of feminist ideology.

Without much qualification, it may be concluded that in scope and sophistication of analysis, feminist ideology had developed as fully by 1844 as it would until the post-World War II period. This is not to say that women no longer thought about the greater questions of "what is woman" and "how can woman best achieve her potential." Rather their focus and energy was directed toward achieving the concrete goal of suffrage. During the period from 1850 to 1920, while several important works on women were published, none were innovative. Those works that may be classified as feminist ideology merely expanded the depth of analysis of earlier feminist ideologists, updated feminist ideology to include evolving events within the women's movement, especially within the area of strategies for change, or incorporated new scientific ideologies and modes of thought that altered perceptions of what a "human being" was and how best to analyze the human condition. Other feminist ideological works merely coalesced the views and interpretations of earlier feminist ideologists. Discussion of a representative sample of the most important of these works and their impact on the evolution of feminist ideology follows.

TRANSITION: IDEOLOGY TO ACTIVISM

The last feminist ideologist to broach the question of woman's nature, Elizabeth Oakes Smith, may be considered a transitionary figure between the earlier feminist ideologists and the later activists, who were only secondarily concerned with a feminist ideology. Elizabeth Oakes Smith belonged to the Transcendentalist circle, although she was not as important a member as Fuller. Oakes Smith was a "Lyceum" lecturer between 1851 and 1857, along with Horace Greeley and Emerson, among others. She knew and commented continuously on the works of Margaret Fuller, often visited Emerson's home, and attended lectures and meetings with members of the Transcendentalist group. In her autobiography she recalled her days with the Transcendentalists. "The days passed with Emerson, Alcott, Thoreau and other Transcendentalists were the breathings of ambrosia."[1]

Oakes Smith's work, *Woman and Her Needs* (1851), combined Fuller's concern for woman's essence and her own recognition of the need for action to replace oratory, with special concern for achieving suffrage and equality. Oakes Smith, as she liked to be called, argued that an awareness of a "wrong" identified through an ideology required action to right it. "From the moment that an individual or a class of individuals, in any community, have become conscious of a series of grievances demanding redress, from that moment they are morally bound to make that conviction vital in action, and to do what in them lies to correct such abuses."[2]

In her analysis of woman's status in society and her prescriptions for improving this status, Oakes Smith closely approximated Fuller's feminist ideology. The similarities between the two ideologies are not surprising given the similar intellectual backgrounds of Fuller and Oakes Smith. In addition to being a Transcendentalist, Oakes Smith was also well read in European philosophies and ideologies. Of special appeal to her were the liberal and radical British ideologies of the late eighteenth and early nineteenth centuries, particularly the Radical Reformers and Utilitarians. She was also well versed in feminist thought and particularly revered Frances Wright for her advocacy of female equality.

Like most earlier ideologists, Oakes Smith concluded that throughout history man had made woman a creature of luxury. Woman failed to undertake unique thought and action by merely fulfilling the roles that man defined for her. Oakes Smith, like Fuller, believed that woman had an unattained potential and function in society. She viewed woman as possessing unique qualities that made her better qualified than man to institute social reform and societal improvement. For Fuller, woman's unique quality was femality. For Oakes Smith, woman's uniqueness was found in "woman thought."

Woman thought, like femality, was the special intuitive power of woman that rendered her better equipped than man to perceive the truths of the universe. Man was blinded by tradition and an overemphasis on reason. Oakes Smith defined woman thought as "a woman-perception, a woman-intuition, altogether distinct from the same things in the other sex; and to learn what these are, and to act from these, is what woman must learn."[3] Because of this intuition and unadulterated status in society, Oakes Smith believed that woman should initiate the moral reformation of the world. "Hers is to be the great birth of a purer humanity, that of peace and love and good will; the embodied testimony of love."[4]

In her prescriptions for woman's future status in society, Oakes Smith's ideology continued to combine components of earlier feminist ideologies. Oakes Smith emphasized the importance of woman's development and the definition of woman's unique character through utilitarian behavior. "The laws of stubborn utilitarianism must govern us; while they may be as fantastic as they please."[5] Approximating Fuller's stance toward marriage, Oakes Smith also claimed that woman should be free not to marry. Both Fuller and Oakes Smith were highly critical of the societal pressures and socialization processes that coerced woman to marry as a matter of course rather than as a rationally chosen life-style. Oakes Smith's criticisms of marriage, however, were more complex than those of earlier feminists. While Fuller denounced the means by which woman entered marriage, Oakes Smith opposed both the form and legal basis of marriage. She believed that marriage should be a contractual relationship between man and woman that would possess the same legal status as any contract between two individuals. Marriage, as a contract, would necessitate the equality of the contractors and free consent in entering into the contract. "In other words, there should be equality—the parties should be of age—and no girl should be considered competent to enter into such contract, unless she has reached her majority in law."[6]

This recommendation for a contractual marriage relationship was a unique development in feminist prescriptions. It expanded Fuller's recommendation for freedom of entry into marriage, and it significantly deviated from earlier feminists' views of woman's improvement being necessary for making woman a better wife and mother. In fact, an analysis of discussions involving the marriage relationship from Wollstonecraft to Oakes Smith reveals the significant development of feminist ideology in the intervening sixty years. Wollstonecraft emphasized female improvement in order to make women better wives. Elizabeth Oakes Smith viewed marriage merely as an option, one alternative life-style for woman, but by no means a necessity.

Programs for changing woman's status in society also changed significantly from Wollstonecraft's *Vindication* to Oakes Smith's *Woman and Her Needs*. While earlier feminists advocated either man assuming responsibility for improving the status of woman or woman using whatever freedom she possessed to improve herself, Oakes Smith's strategy reflected the events of her time. Oakes Smith concluded that the women's movement should and would be the mechanism to achieve woman's equality. Once equality was reached, woman would meet her potential.

Oakes Smith, in summary, advanced few innovations in the development of feminist ideology. Like earlier feminists, she lacked the philosophical acuteness and sophistication of Fuller and contributed nothing new to the philosophical basis of feminist ideology other than redefining Fuller's "femality" as "woman thought." Despite her intellectual training as a Transcendentalist, Oakes Smith's approach to feminism was more activist and practical than theoretical. She dared woman to "know thyself."

Yet Oakes Smith still made two important contributions to feminist ideology, each obviously evolving from her Transcendentalist perspective. First, she advocated the elimination of traditional marriage structures. Her prescription for marriage contracts clearly extended Fuller's advocacy of complete freedom for woman to develop herself. Oakes Smith perceived a marriage contract as vital to woman's individuality, self-fulfillment, and freedom of soul. Second, Oakes Smith contended that woman's societal equality was prerequisite for self-fulfillment and that woman should equalize her own societal position. Identifying the woman's movement of the mid-nineteenth century as the best means for changing woman's status, Oakes Smith concluded that man was too bound by tradition to improve woman's status. Anyway, each individual was responsible for improving humanity.

Thus, Oakes Smith, unlike Fuller and Wright, was part of the new women's suffrage movement both because of her activism within the movement as a lecturer and because of her ideology. She was the beginning of a new generation of feminists—a generation concerned more with practical political achievements than with the intellectual and philosophical development of analyses of woman and woman's status.

Another member of this new generation of feminists, although not an activist herself, was the Englishwoman Harriet Taylor Mill.[7] Her work, *The Enfranchisement of Women*, both lauded the evolving women's suffrage movements and included an excellent summary of feminist ideology. Mill devoted most of her analysis to discussing what the extent of female equality should be, an analysis that closely approximated Sarah Grimké's advocacy of political, legal, and economic equality. But Mill also described woman's nature or essence in a way that was almost identical to Fuller's discussion of femality as the impulsive and instinctual nature of woman. Mill's contribution to the development of feminist ideology, however, rested in neither these analyses of woman's status, prescriptions, nor programs, but rather in her defense of female equality against the increasingly negative response of men to the women's movement and women's suffrage. Like Oakes Smith, Mill's feminist analysis was part of the new feminist generation.

In the *Enfranchisement* Mill delineated six predominant male arguments against female equality and disproved them. The arguments as Mill defined them were: (1) female inequality was an historical custom and tradition; (2) woman was not fit for politics; (3) maternity disqualified woman from equality; (4) woman's economic equality would depress the economy resulting in lower wages; (5) equality would debase woman; and (6) woman did not want equality.

Mill's refutations of these arguments were short and interrelated. First, she asserted that female inequality became a custom and tradition solely through man's superior physical strength. Woman's physical inferiority to man did not mean that she was unfit for politics, however. In fact, like many feminists before her, Mill argued that the successful queens who ruled great nations throughout history proved that if a woman were trained for politics she could compete equally with men within the political sphere.

Second, Mill vehemently attacked the argument that maternity rendered woman unequal to man because it presupposed that motherhood should be the only important role in woman's life. Yet, as Mill contended,

> There is no inherent reason or necessity that all women should voluntarily choose to devote their lives to one animal function and its consequences. Numbers of women are wives and mothers only because there is no other career open to them, no other occupation for their feelings or their activities. Every improvement in their education and enlargement of their faculties, everything which renders them more qualified for any other mode of life, increases the number of those to whom it is an injury and an oppression to be denied the choice. To say that women must be excluded from active life because maternity disqualifies them for it, is in fact to say that every other career should be forbidden them, in order that maternity may be their only resource.[8]

The causal relationship between female equality and female de-

basement that men defined also was an important point of contention for Mill. Keeping woman away from the evil influence of
society would not keep her pure and innocent, as men asserted,
but would perpetuate woman's weakness. It was this misinterpreta-
tion of weakness as innocence that concerned all earlier feminists.
Mill similarly objected to "the plea that women do not desire any
change . . . which is generally not true, and, when true, only so
because there is not that hope of success, without which complaint
seldom makes itself audible to unwilling ears."[9]

The final argument against female equality that Mill countered,
somewhat unsuccessfully, was that woman's economic equality
would depress the economy and subsequently lower wages. Mill
avoided the issue of the detrimental economic effects of woman's
employment and instead proposed that economic equality had no
relevance for suffrage and political equality.

> It is urged, that to give the same freedom of occupation to women as
> to men, would be an injurious addition to the crowd of competitors,
> by whom the avenues of almost all kinds of employment are choked
> up, and its remuneration depressed. This argument, it is to be ob-
> served, does not reach the political question. It gives no excuse for
> withholding from women the rights of citizenship. The suffrage, the
> jury-box, admission to the legislature, and to office, it does not
> touch. It bears only on the industrial branch of the subject.[10]

While Mill was not an important feminist ideologist because she
failed to contribute uniquely to the content of feminism, she still
warrants mention as a contributor to feminist ideology. Mill's
feminism took the form of "applied ideology." She organized existing feminist ideas into a defense, justification, and history of feminism and the women's suffrage movement. In the latter part of the
nineteenth century, such ideological justifications and histories
predominated in feminist writings, while philosophical feminist
writings almost disappeared. Mill's *The Enfranchisement of Women*
thus may be interpreted as a precursor of later feminist histories
and justifications of suffrage. Addresses, speeches, and articles by
activists, such as Elizabeth Cady Stanton, Susan B. Anthony, Lucy
Stone, and Lucretia Mott, were later examples. In fact, feminist
ideology as it evolved in the late eighteenth and early nineteenth

centuries ceased to be generated by feminist activists. In the second half of the nineteenth century and the beginning of the twentieth, a new type of feminist analysis arose—specialized social and economic evaluations of woman's status in society.

In these new social and economic analyses feminists sought to document historically woman's status in society. They delineated the various social and economic roles that woman had played throughout history by relying on newly developed social science theories and methodologies. In other words, their studies included neither analyses of why man subjugated woman, nor reasons why woman should be equal to man, nor any definition of "what is woman." As descriptive rather than analytical interpretations of woman's status in society, these later feminist works defined the "woman condition" as woman's relationship to society, not as the essence of being a woman, as Margaret Fuller had done some years earlier.

The first descriptive work on woman's societal status was published by Caroline H. Dall in 1861, and entitled *The College, The Market, and the Court; or Woman's Relation to Education, Labor and Law.* In *The College,* Dall explained woman's relationship to society in three crucial areas—education, the marketplace, and the legal system. Her descriptions of woman in each of these areas extended from woman's initial entry to woman's status in the mid-nineteenth century. Compared to later descriptions detailing woman's status in only one of these areas, for example, in economics and politics, Dall's work was much broader and hence, given the limit of length, more general. Yet Dall's *The College* was still significant as one of the first works to delineate in detail the factual history of woman's social condition and her evolutionary equality.

Dall's discussion of woman's social condition began with "the college," or the educational opportunities open to woman. Unlike earlier feminists, Dall extended her prescriptions for woman beyond educational equality with man by defining education and the choice of a vocation as *rights* inherent to all human beings. Woman's right to education and a vocation meant that woman should be free to pursue any training and career without legislative or other restrictions. "We have already said, that the educational rights of women are simply those of all human beings."[11]

Woman's right to education included woman's right to an equal education which, Dall believed, could only be obtained through coeducation.[12] Without coeducation, Dall feared, the quality of woman's education would be unequal to man's. To support this opinion, she cited numerous examples of unequal educational facilities in terms of buildings and textbooks and the incompetent teachers who traditionally taught women. Why, throughout history, had woman been educated unequally, both in quality of instruction and subject matter? Dall's answer was simple. Public opinion demanded too little of woman.

Public opinion, a product of history, funcitoned to keep woman subjugated, educationally and otherwise, to the extent that it was only the "noble" and independent who were able to overcome its powerful dictates. The primary source of a public opinion derogatory to woman was history itself.

> The existing public opinion with regard to woman has been formed by the influence of heathen ages and institutions, kept up by a mistaken study of the classics,—a study so pursued, that Athens and Rome, Aristophanes and Juvenal, are more responsible.for the popular views of woman, and for the popular mistakes in regard to man's position toward her, than anything that has been written later.[13]

The ancient precept that woman was inferior distorted both male and female perceptions of woman's potential and her place in society. Modern societal institutions and laws incorporated distinctions between male and female that were based not in logic or rational thought but in misconceptions of the true nature of woman and the true relationship between man and woman. In brief, man's perspectival bias toward woman, assimilated from ancient history, distorted not only the development of contemporary society but the writing and content of history itself.

> If men start with the idea that woman is an inferior being, incapable of wide interests, and created for their pleasure alone; if they enact laws and establish customs to sustain these views; if, for the most part, they shut her into harems, consider her so dangerous that she may not walk the streets without a veil,—they will write history in

accordance with such views, and, whatever may be the facts, they will be interpreted to suit them. They will dwell upon the lives which their theories explain: they will touch lightly or ignore those that puzzle them.[14]

The difficulty that woman consequently confronted in achieving an education equal to man's was overcoming the male and female perspectival biases against woman inculcated by society. The only means for woman to achieve equal education was by achieving self-respect and learning self-help. Realizing that this strategy of self-improvement was a questionable method because it unrealistically assumed that woman would develop the insight and courage to overcome societal biases when she was subject to these biases herself, Dall included a chapter in *The College* entitled, "The Meaning of Lives that Have Modified Public Opinion." In this chapter, Dall cited examples of women who achieved the independence of thought necessary to transcend societal biases. Specifically, she lauded Mary Wollstonecraft, Charlotte Bronte, and Margaret Fuller, among others, as proof of woman's ability to help herself. Despite this chapter, however, Dall failed to come to terms with the issue of how masses of women would overcome societal biases. Although she recognized women who achieved independence of thought, Dall did not attempt to examine how they achieved independence. Similarly, although she accurately identified how perspectival biases functioned to sustain woman's inequality, especially in education, she failed to suggest any means for checking the impact of historically based biases and public opinion. This failure was one example of the descriptive rather than analytical quality of Dall's work.

The second section of *The College, The Market, and The Court* dealt with woman's relationship to the marketplace. In this discussion of woman's economic status, Dall reiterated analyses and conclusions made by earlier feminists, in particular Harriet Taylor Mill. The preponderant innovation that Dall made to the body of literature analyzing woman's economic role was her appeal to diverse cultures, such as Muslim culture, to substantiate the claims that she shared with earlier feminists.

Initially, Dall began this section with the declaration that woman possessed valid claims to equal rights to labor, vocation, and compensation. "I ask for woman, then, free, untrammelled access to all fields of labor."[15] Dall concluded that human nature, to be fully developed, necessitated labor. Woman must work not only to support herself and her family in some instances, of which Dall cited a multiplicity of examples, but also because it was vital to human development. Idleness to Dall led to moral degradation and physical degeneration.[16] This claim, of course, repeated claims made by feminists since Wollstonecraft.

After proclaiming woman's right to equal labor, Dall proceeded to counter male objections to this equality by citing diverse cultural examples of woman's successful performance as a laborer. First, she scrutinized the argument that woman was unfit for physically demanding employment. "Women have, from the beginning, done the hardest and most unwholesome work of the world in all countries, whether civilized or uncivilized; and I am prepared to prove it."[17] Another objection to woman entering the labor force was an issue that Mill skirted, that woman would depress wages. Dall, however, confronted this objection directly. "Do you assert that, if all avenues were thrown open, it would not increase the quantity of work; and that there would be more laborers in consequence, and lower wages for all? Lower wages for *some*, I reply; but certainly higher wages for women; and they too, would be raised to the rank of partners."[18] Depression of wages resulting from woman's entry into the labor force was, however, only symptomatic of a larger problem. Woman's entry into a healthy capitalistic system should not depress wages at all. The real cause was the "want of respect for labor." If labor were properly respected, wages would be higher regardless of woman's entry into the labor market.

The ultimate solution to the problem of equality of labor in Dall's analysis was equal compensation for equal work and equal employment opportunities for all classes of women, rich and poor alike. The easiest way for women to earn equal wages was for them to establish their own workshops.[19] Both of these strategies would increase respect for woman and woman's labor. But fundamentally for Dall, woman's right to equal labor should be established in law, the law of custom as well as the law of courts.

Caroline Dall's contentions for equal legal rights for woman, which she expressed as "civil rights," were also expounded in her discussion of "The Court." In this area Dall reiterated arguments made by earlier feminist ideologists and activists that woman should possess equal citizenship with man. "You are, then, to base your demand for woman's civil rights upon her simple humanity,—the value of the soul itself. If you deny this foundation for her, you deny it for yourselves, and the Declaration of Independence is only an impertinent pretence."[20]

Drawing upon historical examples from Europe and America, Dall summarized woman's history as a noncitizen, with her lack of civil and legal rights under all governments since the Roman Empire. She particularly denounced marriage and property laws, which rendered the married woman a slave to her husband economically and legally. She was concerned about woman's lack of suffrage and the other rights and duties of citizenship. Most of Dall's section on "The Court" was thus a reconsideration of the predominate claims of earlier feminist ideologists and the suffragists.

Her one unique contribution to the content of feminist analyses of woman's legal status was her condemnation of laws that undermined the civil and legal status of the single woman.

In the laws which regard single women, we object, then,—
1. To the withholding of the elective franchise.
2. To the law's preference of males, and the issue of males in the division of estates.
3. We object to the estimate of woman which the law sustains, which shuts her out from all public employment, for many branches of which she is better fitted than man.
4. We object to that estimate of woman's chastity which makes its existence or non-existence of importance only as it affects the comfort or income of man.[21]

The claim of equal rights for the single woman was mentioned by Margaret Fuller but was understandably of more importance for Dall. While Fuller stated that woman should be free to choose bachelorhood rather than marry, Dall identified laws that precluded a single woman's equality with man. In this way Dall updated Fuller's freedom to be single to include a newly arising class of single women who needed legal protection and who deserved legal equality.

Dall's work, *The College, The Market, and The Court* was, in summary, a good example of the descriptive statements of woman's historical social position that evolved in the late nineteenth and early twentieth centuries. Dall's overview of woman's educational, economic, and civil (legal) status was broader than most such descriptions. Yet *The College* exemplified the feminist writings that evolved to support and justify the woman's suffrage movement in its descriptive, rather than analytical, orientation. Most feminist writings from the mid-nineteenth century, when Dall wrote *The College*, until the post-World War II period followed this descriptive format. They described and summarized woman's social condition both before and after the passage of the woman's suffrage amendment. Despite the notoriety of some of these feminist authors, few of their works merit mention as they merely reiterated feminist analyses made decades earlier.

These later feminist works were different from Dall's only in that they were more specialized descriptions of a single aspect of woman's social condition, specializations due to either the utilization of new perspectives and methodologies of the developing social sciences— economic theory, historical method, sociology, and anthropology— or to their reliance upon new political ideologies, such as anarchism and new forms of socialism. In most instances, the later feminists also focused on only one aspect of woman's social condition, such as the economic, legal, or social roles. It is important to reemphasize, however, that, like Dall, none of these later feminists considered the greater philosophical questions of woman's human condition, her undiscovered potential, or her "essence." The feminist analyses of the late nineteenth and early twentieth centuries solely considered woman's social condition, how woman's societal roles had evolved and how they could be changed to render woman equal to man. None of these analyses require a detailed discussion here because of their repetitive content, but a few should be mentioned to indicate the breadth of topics covered and the perspectives employed in analysis.

In 1898, Charlotte Perkins Gilman, who may be described as a socialistic sociologist, published *Women and Economics: A Study of the Economic Relation Between Men and Women as a Factor in Social Evolution*. In *Women and Economics,* Gilman defined woman's economic status as dependent upon the sex relation between man and woman. She concluded that society possessed an "androcentric culture," or, in other words, "that one sex should have monopolized all human activities, called them 'man's work,' and managed them as such."[22] Only by eliminating sex as the social and economic determinant of male and female roles could woman become equal. Woman's equality depended upon the establishment of socialistic social and economic roles for woman. The family and home should be dissolved, and new institutions, such as communal kitchens, professional housekeepers, and day nurseries for children, should be instituted in their place.

Anna Garlin Spencer, who published *Woman's Share in Social Culture* in 1912, disagreed with Gilman's socialist alternative for woman, but undertook a similar analysis of woman's social condition. Also a sociologist, Spencer traced the evolution of woman's societal roles from the birth of civilization. Like earlier feminists, she argued that woman's social condition—in economics, education, and under the law—should be identical to man's. Her method of achieving equality was through woman's suffrage.

> Women must be given the duty and responsibility, as well as the protection and the power of the ballot, in order that there may be established a free, recognized and obvious channel by which the value of women's contribution to the State may be conserved and effectively applied to social welfare.[23]

Later well-known feminist writings of the twentieth century included, among others, those of the anarchist Emma Goldman, whose essays "The Traffic in Women" (1910) and "Marriage and Love" focused on prostitution as exemplary of the exploitation of all women and on marriage as an economic relationship, respectively. In 1920, in *Woman and the New Race*, Margaret Sanger asserted that birth control was an important step toward increasing woman's freedom because motherhood should be voluntary. The majority of feminist works of this period emulated the pattern of Goldman's and Sanger's works. They focused on one facet of woman's relationship to society and offered prescriptions and strategies within this one area. Because of their narrow focus, they cannot be classified as ideology as defined in this study—sets of beliefs about how society is organized and functions and prescriptions for changing woman's roles and power within society.

In summary, when looking at twentieth-century feminist writings before the beginning of the contemporary women's movement, we find that they contributed little to the development of feminism as an ideology. Feminist ideology as it existed until the post-World War II period was formulated in the nineteenth century. The development of feminist ideology, its evaluations of women's status in society, prescriptions for change, and strategies for achieving change were all rooted in the changing socioeconomic and political environments of nineteenth-century Europe and America.

FEMINIST IDEOLOGY BEFORE WORLD WAR II

A composite of feminist ideology as it existed before World War II may be constructed by combining important components of individual feminists' thought that survived within feminism until the mid-twentieth century. In developing such a composite of feminist ideology, the sources of the major ideas and components of feminism also may be identified. Constructing this composite, however, poses some problems, the major problem being the distortion of the relative importance of individual feminist ideologists. Since it is much easier for any thinker to build on the ideas of a predecessor than to construct a new mode of thought or analysis, later thinkers delineated more sophisticated ideologies. Important early feminists, such as Mary Wollstonecraft, thus contributed less to a composite of feminist ideology as it existed in the early twentieth century than later feminists who built upon her thought. Still, in the evaluations of woman's status in society made by feminists over the years, the following analyses of woman's relationships to society and roles and power within society survived. Each analysis may be included as a component of a composite of feminist ideology on the basis of its being generally accepted by later feminists as an important analysis.

Of importance for all feminists was woman's lack of equal intellectual abilities with man. Woman lacked equal intellect because she possessed unequal educational opportunities, both in quality and scope of education. Wollstonecraft's basic presumption in the *Vindication* was that woman was irrational and unable to reason primarily because she lacked education. Wollstonecraft's concern with woman's lack of intellectual development continued throughout the development of feminist ideology. Frances Wright attributed woman's lack of political rights to her lack of intellectual capabilities and education. Wright argued that without education to develop the intellect no human being could participate in a democratic society. Political rights required intellectual development.

Sarah Grimké defined woman's unequal intellect more fully than her predecessors. Grimké asserted that woman's unequal intellect was not innate (a fact of which Wollstonecraft was not too sure) but a result of poor education. If woman's education were improved, her intellect would also improve. In Grimké's words, "intellect is not sexed." Mid-nineteenth-century feminist ideologists generally, however, developed their discussions of woman's intellect along the lines that Wright first established. For Margaret Fuller and later ideologists, lack of intellectual ability due to poor education meant that woman could not partake equally with man of the political, economic, and social rights inherent in a democratic state.

Fuller's concern with woman's self-realization and the fulfillment of woman's potential (her complete intellectual development) has predominated as a concern of feminists until the present. Woman's undeveloped intellect rendered it impossible for woman to know herself and realize the limits, strengths, and weaknesses of both her abilities and her nature. This lack of intellectual development, in Fuller's analysis, resulted in a lack of internal freedom for woman in all aspects of human existence—intellectual, moral, and spiritual. In other words, without a developed intellect, woman was unable to think for herself. Feminist ideologists from the mid-nineteenth to the mid-twentieth century believed that if woman acquired an education equal to man's, then woman would realize her potential and nature. As both Oakes Smith and Fuller concluded, woman then would know what it meant to be a woman, the first step toward self-respect and self-reliance.

Woman's lack of intellectual development and poor education rendered her unequal in almost all aspects of societal life—political, legal, economic, and social. Flora Tristan first concluded that woman lacked occupational and professional rights. Sarah Grimké expanded this analysis to conclude that woman received unequal pay for equal work, an observation made in reaction to woman's entry into the industrial labor force. Wright and Tristan, the socialists, concluded that woman lacked the political rights inherent in a democracy, particularly the right to vote. Grimké expanded the definition of woman's lack of political rights from the lack of suffrage to include woman's exclusion from policy making and the execution of law.

Fuller and Elizabeth Oakes Smith were the first feminist ideologists concerned with woman's rights in marriage, not merely as wives and mothers, but the nature of the marriage relationship itself. Fuller proposed that women should be free not to marry. Oakes Smith developed this line of thought much more fully, concluding that woman's inequality within the marriage relationship could only be eliminated by a radical revision of the legal basis of marriage. For Oakes Smith, marriage should be a contractual relationship between two equal partners.

Caroline Dall's most important contribution to criticisms of woman's status in society was in none of these areas. Dall, writing in the mid-nineteenth century, was concerned with the new class of woman that industrial society had created—the single working (or career) woman. While the single woman performed man's work, she was accorded none of the legal, political, or economic rights that man possessed, for example, in taxation and working conditions.

Beliefs about the causes of these inequalities in woman's status were fundamentally the same for all developers of feminist ideology. The most important cause was man. From Wollstonecraft's analysis of male tyranny, man's desire to subjugate woman predominated as the primary cause of woman's inequality in the feminists' analyses. By writing history and creating public opinion, in Dall's ideology, as well as by creating and then enforcing the law, as all earlier feminists mentioned, man erased woman's desires for self-improvement and equality. Feminist ideology early in its development acknowledged that one of the most powerful obstacles to woman's equality was her contentment with her lot.

The social institution that nineteenth-century feminist ideologists credited with being responsible both for male tyranny over woman and for woman's lack of desire for further equality was religion.

Beginning with Wright, feminist ideologists criticized religion for working to keep woman inferior by emphasizing woman's creation from Adam's rib and woman's inferior moral status.

But Sarah Grimké identified the most important force in keeping woman inferior. It was the force that pervaded religion and regulated male and female attitudes toward woman—sexism. Sexual differentiation—the classification, characterization, and categorization of human beings on the basis of sex rather than capabilities and potential—was the primary cause of woman's inequality for Grimké and all later feminist ideologists.

The prescriptions that feminist ideologists developed historically for changing and improving woman's status in society reflected their criticisms of woman's existing condition. Each feminist, in defining future roles and power for woman within society, delineated prescriptions that would ameliorate the inequities that she identified in society. Economic inequality should be replaced by equality, the lack of political rights with equal rights, and so on. Thus, for each inequity that the feminist ideologists identified, they prescribed a solution.

Specifically, the primary concern of all the ideologists was woman's independence from man. Margaret Fuller first advocated total independence in the mid-nineteenth century. Independence for Fuller encompassed not only the roles and rights of woman but also woman's psychological independence from man. The source of this independence was education.

Equal education for woman became an issue initially for Mary Wollstonecraft. Wollstonecraft asserted that woman's education should suffice to develop woman's intellect and reason as much as possible. The only feasible means of achieving woman's intellectual development was to provide her with an education equal to that of man. While Wollstonecraft failed to define fully what she meant by an equal education, Wright provided a definition. Equal education for Wright meant equality of educational opportunity as well as equality of instruction. Equal education later in the nineteenth century, as in Dall's analysis, meant coeducation.

Another important prescription for early feminist ideologists that persisted into the twentieth century was equality in marriage.

Although first defined by Frances Wright as equal property and divorce laws, by the mid-nineteenth century equal rights in marriage came to mean a marriage contract. In Elizabeth Oakes Smith's analysis, woman could achieve equality in marriage only if it was a legal contract identical to any other legal contract between two individuals. A marriage contract necessitated freedom of entry into marriage by individuals who were in complete control of their faculties, of age, and who were considered equal.

Long before Oakes Smith's work, however, feminists had prescribed complete equality for woman in all areas of life. Flora Tristan in the early nineteenth century made the first such claim. While Tristan merely defined complete equality in general terms, such as civil, political, and economic equality, later feminists quickly specified areas and ways in which equality should be achieved. For instance, Margaret Fuller expanded economic equality to mean equal employment opportunities for woman in an era when women were given the most unskilled and lowest paid jobs in the evolving industrial state. In the mid-nineteenth century, Caroline Dall extended economic equality to mean the right to a vocation, the right to labor, the right to equal pay for equal work, and the right of equal taxation on earned income.

Generally, though, by the late 1830s, feminists, most notably Grimké, had restricted themselves to advocating complete equality for woman in all areas of life in lieu of less comprehensive recommendations for equality. It is interesting to note that within forty years after Wollstonecraft had advocated predominately educational equality for woman so that she might be a better wife and mother, feminist ideologists were demanding unequivocal equality.

The programs for achieving change that feminist ideologists delineated prior to the contemporary women's movement underwent the greatest alteration and confusion in development and acceptance. Early feminists, such as Wollstonecraft, posited that equal education was the most efficacious means of achieving equality. The emphasis on education was quickly replaced, however, by the pre-Marxian socialist feminists, such as Wright and Tristan, who believed that only a total restructuring of society along socialist lines could transform society and render woman truly equal. Yet, by the late 1830s, education as a strategy reemerged to replace the socialist vision. Grimké and Fuller both strongly asserted that education was a prerequisite for equality. Once woman achieved equality in education, she would be able to win her own equality.

Thus, before the women's suffrage movement established itself in the mid-nineteenth century, feminist ideologists had repudiated any male role in achieving woman's equality. They emphasized that woman should free herself. By 1850, feminist ideologists were advocating the women's suffrage movement as the most feasible means for achieving equality. Elizabeth Oakes Smith, herself an activist, and Harriet Taylor Mill first justified woman's activism as the best road to equality.

The reliance upon the women's suffrage movement to achieve female equality did not remain the only strategy defined within feminist ideology for long. By the late nineteenth century, the increase in new post-Marxian socialist movements in Europe and America led to a reversion to the strategies of the earlier utopian socialists. Charlotte Perkins Gilman demanded a socialist restructuring of society, particularly the socialization of woman's roles and positions within society. But these late nineteenth- and early twentieth-century socialists influenced the development of feasible programs within feminist ideology no more than had their utopian predecessors. The thrust of feminist strategies during this period remained the suffrage movement. This group included the new social scientists, few of whom were ideologists, of whom Anna Garlin Spencer was representative.

With the passage of the women's suffrage amendment in 1920, however, the development of strategies for achieving equality for woman ended, as did many new developments in the evolution of feminist ideology. In fact, as this composite of the major developments and contributions to feminist ideology illustrates, feminist ideology had developed as fully by the mid-nineteenth century as it would until the contemporary women's movement.

For example, in analyzing the criticisms and evaluations of woman's status in society, we find that feminist ideologists by 1861 (the publication of Caroline Dall's work) criticized woman's status in all spheres of societal life and included all classes of women—

the upper and middle classes, female slaves, workers, and the newest class, the single career woman. Woman's inequality in the economic, legal, civil, educational, political, and religious spheres and within social relationships, such as marriage and the family, were carefully documented. Woman's own individual development had also been analyzed in detail by Margaret Fuller and others. Similarly, beginning with Mary Wollstonecraft, the sources and causes of woman's inequality and how they functioned had been conscientiously evaluated.

Prescriptions for future roles and power for woman within society had also developed as much by the mid-nineteenth century as they would until the post-World War II period. Sarah Grimké's prescription for complete equality in all areas of life for woman accomplished this function. The strategies of a socialist reconstruction of society and the women's suffrage movement, the only two strategies to evolve during this period, had also been defined before 1860.

While the preceding composite of feminist ideology merely highlights the major arguments of the pre-World War II period, it illustrates that feminist ideology had evolved to its most complete stage in all three elements of ideology—evaluations of society, prescriptions, and programs for change—by the mid-nineteenth century. The composite also demonstrates that feminist ideology evolved by a process of later feminists building upon the ideas and theories of earlier feminists. For example, while Wollstonecraft was concerned with woman's role within the marriage relationship, Fuller and Oakes Smith redefined woman's role in this area as being one of choice and contractual, respectively. In the areas of prescriptions and programs, the same refinement and clarification of components of feminist ideology over time may be identified. Political rights, which were virtually absent from Wollstonecraft's prescriptions, for instance, were soon expanded by others to mean the right to vote and, eventually, complete political equality and equal political rights. Programs for change similarly developed from woman asking man to equalize her status to the self-help strategy of the women's suffrage movement.

It is therefore correct to conclude that although feminist thought lacked a single major proponent in the pre-World War II period and although no one thinker ever comprehensively summarized the components of feminist thought as it evolved over the years, feminist thought may be considered "ideology." As it evolved over time and was continuously expanded upon and developed, feminist ideology had come into existence as early as the mid-nineteenth century.

NOTES

1. Elizabeth Oakes Smith, in Mary Alice Wyman, ed., *Selections from the Autobiography of Elizabeth Oakes Smith* (Lewiston, Me.: Lewiston Journal Company, 1924), p. 140.

2. Mrs. E. Oakes Smith, *Woman and Her Needs* (New York: Fowlers and Wells, 1851), p. 1.

3. Ibid., p. 23.

4. Ibid., p. 24.

5. Ibid., pp. 102-03.

6. Ibid., p. 53.

7. The contributions of Mill to feminist ideology and thought are a matter of controversy among contemporary political theorists. Several works on women and their status in society were written by John Stuart Mill and/or Harriet Taylor, later Mrs. Mill. But the authorship of many of the works cannot be established definitively. Works published in the 1830s on marriage and divorce are usually credited to John Stuart Mill, as is the later *The Subjection of Women*, despite his assertions that *Subjection* was a product of Mrs. Mill's genius. The "Enfranchisement of Women," however, first published in the *Westminister Review* in 1851, usually is accepted as the work of Harriet Taylor Mill. The analysis of Harriet Taylor Mill as a feminist ideologist that follows is thus based solely on this work.

8. Harriet Taylor Mill, "Enfranchisement of Women," *Westminister and Foreign Quarterly Review* (July 1851):7.

9. Ibid., p. 12.

10. Ibid., p. 26.

11. Caroline H. Dall, *The College, The Market, and The Court; or Woman's Relation to Education, Labor and Law* (1886; reprint ed., Boston: Memorial Edition, 1914), p. 6.

12. Ibid., p. 8.

13. Ibid., p. 49.

14. Ibid., p. 61.

15. Ibid., p. 135.

16. Ibid., p. 179.

17. Ibid., p. 156.

18. Ibid., p. 136.

19. Ibid., p. 138.

20. Ibid., p. 373.

21. Ibid., p. 295.

22. Charlotte Perkins Gilman, *Women and Economics: A Study of the Economic Relation Between Men and Women as a Factor in Social Evolution* (Boston: Small, Maynard and Company, 1898), p. 25.

23. Anna Garlin Spencer, *Woman's Share in Social Culture* (New York: Mitchell Kennerley, 1912), p. 300.

Contemporary Feminist Ideology

SINCE WORLD WAR II, the feminist movement has produced a plethora of analytical treatises on woman's status in society. The resurgence of feminism and feminist thought in this period may be attributed to three major factors. First, the impact of the Civil Rights movement on women and woman's growing involvement in that movement encouraged woman to speak for herself. Second, the Vietnam War protests, which radicalized young people across America in the 1960s, provided an example of political action for feminists. And, third, throughout the 1960s the developing political and social consciousness of exploited people everywhere—American blacks and Native Americans, Southeast Asians, and the Third World—generally encouraged women to think of themselves as exploited.

The person most often credited by contemporary feminists with awakening woman's consciousness in the period since World War II is Betty Friedan. Not only did Friedan found the National Organization of Women, but she also wrote what most feminists consider to be the first contemporary analysis of woman's status in society. Her book, *The Feminine Mystique*, was an attempt to explain why women in the United States assumed political passivity after winning the vote in 1919, and especially after World War II. Exemplary of the praise Friedan received was that of Germaine Greer, herself the author of the famous treatise on woman, *The Female Eunuch*. "The beginning of the second feminist wave, of which this book must be considered a part, was Betty Friedan's research into the post-war sexual sell which got American women out of the factories and back into their homes."[1]

Although most contemporary feminists credit Friedan with inspiring the contemporary feminist movement, they do not consider her work, *The Feminine Mystique,* an explanation and justification of the movement itself.

> Although feminism has a long history, the contemporary feminist movement is sufficiently new that there is no systematically organized body of the new feminist thought. . . . Although pieces have been written that are already considered "classics" within the movement, there is no single recognized theoretician or theory of the movement. Instead, the theoretical formulations are scattered through a multitude of feminist writings.[2]

Each of these three assertions—that feminism was a product of the 1960s, that Friedan was the founder of contemporary feminism, and that feminism lacks a single theoretician, however, is incorrect. First, the contemporary feminist movement developed long before the beginning of the Vietnam War and the spreading consciousness of Third World exploitation. While contemporary feminism was significantly related to the evolution of the Civil Rights movement, it was not related to the Civil Rights activism of the 1960s, but to the origin of that movement in the 1940s. "Conceptually, Women's Lib is not a revival of the earlier feminist movement, being much more an application to women of the Negro drive which has progressed from Civil Rights to Black Power."[3] Second, Betty Friedan cannot be credited with beginning the second feminist wave. When Friedan's work was published in 1963, women's rights were already a topic of discussion in the United States. The President's Commission on the Status of Women, for example, was established in 1961. And third, the contemporary feminist movement has a single theoretician and a single theory. That theory may be found in *The Second Sex,* and that theoretician is Simone de Beauvoir.

This evaluation of contemporary feminist thought begins at the beginning, with an evaluation of *The Second Sex.* Beauvoir, as the theoretician of contemporary feminism, developed both a new perspective and a new methodology for analyzing woman's status in society which later feminists employed. By 1949, when Beauvoir published *The Second Sex,* the social sciences, and specifically psychology and sociology, provided frameworks (however adequate) for all analyses of society and the individual's relationship to society. The feminists were no exception in utilizing the new social sciences in their analyses.

Because feminist writings of the post-World War II period are numerous and analytically varied, the selection of thinkers for study in addition to Beauvoir required care. The nature of this project offered guidelines for selection. Many feminist thinkers were too action-oriented to be discussed as feminist ideologists. They developed reasons to justify specific actions or courses of activism *after* the action had already occurred. These works obviously could not be discussed as ideology because strategies for change cannot be evaluated if they were implemented before the value systems that should have guided their development were constructed.[4]

Other feminist thinkers were too heavily immersed in the social sciences. While the social sciences have influenced all contemporary feminist thinkers to some extent, including Beauvoir, many feminist analyses of woman were so confined to social science methodologies that the development of an ideology was hindered. Most of these analyses focused on empirically or behaviorally evaluating woman's status in society, such as woman in education, employment, and the legal system. Caroline Bird's *Born Female: The High Cost of Keeping Women Down* is an excellent example of such an analysis. The use of social science methodologies for analyzing woman in society thus severely limited the scope of analyses by focusing on one aspect of the woman condition instead of the broad-based social, political, and economic evaluations that are essential components of ideology. Because such analyses were restricted to drawing conclusions about woman's status from empirical evidence, they did not identify the sources or reasons for that status—again, an important component of any ideology.

This limitation on the scope of feminist analyses was not the only hindrance to the evolution of feminist ideology caused by the social sciences. Generally accepted social science theories (especially behavioral theories) severely restricted the perspectives and foci of contemporary feminist analyses. The specific social science theories, such as Freud's concept of woman's castration complex and Talcott Parsons's concept of social roles, established suppositions about woman that feminists felt compelled to refute. Many feminist thinkers thus devoted too much of their analyses to refuting the theoretical assumptions or assertions of the social scientific works. This inhibited them from offering or developing alternative theories. All of the feminist thinkers analyzed in this chapter fall into this category, although some were able to advance beyond the social sciences to offer partial theories of their own about woman—theories based in social science but not restricted by it. In fact, the feminist thinkers discussed often utilized the methodologies and perspectives of more than one of the social sciences in analyzing woman.

The difficulty of selecting feminists to analyze as representative of the thought of the contemporary women's movement was lessened by the fact that a few feminist thinkers of this period were *most* representative of different types of feminist analyses of woman. Specifically, Simone de Beauvoir was the most important feminist thinker of the post-World War II period. In her work she incorporated virtually all aspects of contemporary feminist analyses. Other representative thinkers discussed in this chapter include the generally acknowledged "classics," the most broad-based analyses of woman: Betty Friedan, *The Feminine Mystique;* Germaine Greer, *The Female Eunuch;* and Elizabeth Janeway, *Man's World, Woman's Place.* Other works that are mentioned only briefly because they were either too restricted to the social sciences or too polemical to be considered ideology are: Shulamith Firestone, *The Dialectic of Sex: The Case for Feminist Revolution;* Juliet Mitchell, *Woman's Estate;* Caroline Bird, *Born Female;* and Viola Klein, *The Feminine Character.* Many other feminist thinkers have developed similar analyses and could be included, but these works are both the most representative and the best known.

SIMONE DE BEAUVOIR: THE THEORETICIAN OF CONTEMPORARY FEMINISM

Simone de Beauvoir is the theoretician of contemporary feminism. Like the early nineteenth-century feminist thinkers, her substantial contributions to the evolution of feminist ideology were a result of her predetermined ideological perspective. Beauvoir's first treatise on women and the most significant for her feminist ideology, *The*

Second Sex, was an application of the philosophy of existentialism to woman's human condition, specifically the existentialism of Jean-Paul Sartre.[5] This application was made consciously by Beauvoir.[6]

Sartrian existentialism proceeded from the assumption that existence precedes essence. Man was born nothing. Only by living was he defined.

> There is no human nature, since there is no God to conceive it. Not only is man what he conceives himself to be, but he is also what he wills himself to be after this thrust toward existence. . . . Man is nothing but what he makes of himself. Such is the first principle of existentialism.[7]

Sartrian existentialism was obviously a philosophy of human nature or, more precisely, a philosophy of the nature of human existence. Sartre's self-made man was a creature who willed or consciously decided what he would be. Man retained full responsibility for his own existence. Because he was aware of what he was and aware that his will made him different from other life forms, man was aware of himself as a being. Sartre referred to this self-awareness, or consciousness, as "pre-reflective *cogito.*"

Yet, while Sartre denied God's determination of man's nature and similarly rejected notions of the formation of character through circumstances, he still conceded that man's freedom was limited. Although man was free to be what he would, he was bounded still by his facticity, his physical being in the real world. Facticity was the totality of the circumstances that bounded man's existence, the situations that he could not control but within which he made decisions and exercised his consciousness. "How we experience our circumstances, how we allow them to influence our outlook, our language, the kinds of assumptions we make and the values we assign to things—all these things are within our power to choose."[8]

Man as a conscious being bounded by his facticity possessed for Sartre three states of being. First, the state of Being-In-itself was the self-contained being of a thing. Man was a man. A being was what it was. Since man was born a man, some functions emanating from the condition of being man were predetermined, for example, life functions. But above all, a Being-In-itself was always consistent with itself.

The second state of being was man as a conscious being—Being-For-itself. In this state man possessed and utilized consciousness. He was free to make decisions by and about himself. The state of Being-For-itself, thus, was the human condition in which man willed what he would be, or in which he existed. As a Being-For-itself, man acted because action was based on projection into the future. He made choices because he possessed the subjective freedom necessary to choose and to give his life meaning. The Being-For-itself, therefore, was in a constant state of transcendence because he was always beyond himself in making choices and acting.

Sartre's third condition of being is the most important for an analysis of Beauvoir's *The Second Sex*. The third state of being, Being-For-others, was the concept in Sartre's existentialism upon which his social philosophy and analyses of the social relationships of men were based. Being-For-others was a "new dimension of Being in which my Self exists outside as an object for others. The For-others involves a perpetual conflict as each For-itself seeks to recover its own Being by directly or indirectly making an object out of the other."[9] Social relations were inherently conflictual. Each Being-For-itself established itself as Subject while defining other Beings as Objects, or Others. Each Being-For-itself thus sought control over other Beings. "While I attempt to free myself from the hold of the Other, the Other is trying to free himself from mine; while I seek to enslave the Other, the Other seeks to enslave me. . . . Descriptions of concrete behavior must be seen within the perspective of *conflict*."[10]

Since each Subject established all other Beings as Others, each Subject developed descriptions of roles for the Other to which the Subject wished the Other to conform. "Every I is essentially a closed entity"[11] because two Subjects, two Beings-For-itself could not be fused into a "harmonious whole." Every Subject, therefore, conceived of itself as essential and transcendent, while the Other was relegated to immanence and inessentialness by the Subject.

In summary, "Man is nothing else than his plan; he exists only to the extent that he fulfills himself; he is therefore nothing else than the ensemble of his acts, nothing else than his life."[12] To fulfill himself, man must be free and a Subject. Man must determine his own life.

In *The Second Sex* Beauvoir analyzed woman's inequality and subjection in society and her lack of internal freedom by utilizing the Sartrian states of being as criteria for evaluating woman's relationship to man. Through the concepts of being, Beauvoir was able to identify the societal forces that controlled woman and the causes and reasons for these forces. This analysis, emanating from her existentialist perspective, was her contribution to feminist ideology.

Elizabeth Janeway recognized the theoretical basis of Beauvoir's analysis of woman.

> "Otherness," as Simone de Beauvoir saw very clearly, implies alienation from power. Women are *The Second Sex* because they are experienced by men as "others," that is, as essentially and inescapably different. It is not possible to be separate and equal, because being separate prevents one from acting in the real world, man's world.[13]

The key to understanding woman's inferiority was recognition of her "Otherness," her immanence, or realizing that woman was an Object and not a Subject. The best way to determine what Beauvoir meant by woman as the "Other" is to investigate her description of how woman became the "Other," inherently different and separate from man.

The first sixth of *The Second Sex* was devoted to evaluating explanations offered by the social and biological sciences for woman's inferior status. Beauvoir rejected all "scientific" theories that purported to explain and often defend woman's inferiority. The "natural hierarchy" or scale of value theories of the biological sciences were correct in nature; that is, woman was physically weaker than man. But physical weakness, Beauvoir argued, was insignificant and should not be employed to justify or explain the inequality of woman in the modern world. Nor should it be used to relegate her to a lower position on the evolutionary scale.

After refuting biological justifications and explanations of woman's inferior social status, Beauvoir turned to the social sciences. Among the most predominant psychological explanations of both woman's inferior status and the reasons underlying woman's demands for equality were Freud's interrelated theories of woman's castration complex and penis envy. Freudians argued that woman accepted inferiority and subservience to man because she recognized man's superiority. Both men and women considered woman castrated. Similarly, those women who sought equality did so because they envied man's superiority. Beauvoir rejected these Freudian explanations of woman's unequal social status. She conceded woman's inferiority complex and envy of man, but not woman's castration complex. Woman's envy was rather a reaction to man's privileges, not to his physical possessions. "The place the father holds in the family, the universal predominance of males, her own education— everything confirms her in her belief in masculine superiority."[14] In fact, Beauvoir argued, the "prestige of the penis is explained by the sovereignty of the father."[15]

Beauvoir, after quickly rejecting these scientific explanations of female inferiority, developed her own analysis of its sources and nature. She began with an analysis of woman's nature in society. By "nature" Beauvoir did not refer to some predetermined character that woman received from God or from the circumstances around her, but her nature or character as it really existed because of her societal roles. Briefly, Beauvoir concluded that woman was the Other in a true Sartrian sense of the word. Woman was the Other in society because man relegated her to that condition and conceived of her as immanence.

In determining the reasons for man's definition of woman as Other, Beauvoir adopted the Sartrian notion of the basic conflictual nature of human relations. She contended that any Being-For-itself sought to control other Beings, both Beings-In-itself and Beings-For-itself. Man established himself as a Being-For-itself, as Subject, because he perceived of himself as creative. He constructed society while woman retained the predetermined biological functions of nature. Thus, man feared woman as he feared nature because both were the unknown. To control his fear, and hence to preserve his freedom, man considered it mandatory to control woman. Like any Being-For-itself as defined by Sartre, consequently, man established woman as Other, as Object, in an attempt to control her. He defined acceptable roles for woman in society and forced her to conform to these roles. "At the moment when man asserts himself as subject and free being, the idea of the Other arises. From that day the relation with the Other is dramatic: the existence of the Other is a threat, a danger."[16]

Woman's inferiority began in primitive society. Woman was the giver of life. But in primitive society, man risked his life to protect others. This was the source of woman's inferiority. Man, the creator of society, controlled the forces of nature. Woman, the human representation of nature, was destined for the "repetition of life." "The human male also remodels the face of the earth, he creates new instruments, he invents, he shapes the future. In setting himself up as a sovereign, he is supported by the complicity of woman herself."[17]

When man began to control nature and therefore separated himself from nature, he separated himself from woman. Woman was nature personified because she gave life without controlling it. When this separation between man and woman occurred, man became free.[18] Since the threat of the potential power of the Other must be eliminated for man to be really free, he controlled woman. This development, for Beauvoir, was the source of woman's inferior status. Man, consciously or subconsciously, was forced to subordinate and control woman in order to preserve his own freedom.

As civilization developed, the forms that male control over woman took became more complicated and powerful. In Beauvoir's analysis, marriage evolved into a coercive structure for continuing woman's inferior status. The married woman throughout history always possessed less freedom than young girls and widows. Man developed a strict morality and strict economic controls for his wife but not for women of the world who led "extremely licentious lives."[19]

In the modern world, after centuries of male control, primarily through the marriage relationship, the female became far removed from her original condition in nature. "Women are still, for the most part, in a state of subjection. It follows that woman sees herself and makes her choices not in accordance with her true nature itself, but as man defines her."[20] And how does man define woman?

Man seeks in woman the Other as Nature and as his fellow being. But we know what ambivalent feelings Nature inspires in man. He exploits her, but she crushes him, he is born of her and dies in her; she is the source of his being and the realm that he subjugates to his will.[21]

Woman as the Other, the source of danger for man to be controlled, permeated all thoughts of man and the structure of society itself. Woman as the Other was, for Beauvoir, a metaphysical idea, a myth upon which man built society. The myth of woman was absolute truth. "It projects into the realm of Platonic ideas a reality that is directly experienced or is conceptualized on a basis of experience; in place of fact, value, significance, knowledge, empirical law, it substitutes a transcendental idea, timeless, unchangeable, necessary."[22]

Man's myth of woman as Other was so pervasive that woman accepted the myth herself. She accepted her Otherness, her inferiority and separateness. This acceptance of Otherness Beauvoir labeled the "Feminine Mystery." "It is necessary for the Other to be for itself an other, for its very subjectivity to be affected by its otherness; this consciousness which would be alienated as a consciousness, in its pure immanent presence, would evidently be Mystery."[23]

After defining woman as Other, Beauvoir utilized the social sciences she earlier criticized to delineate and evaluate the perpetuation of the Feminine Mystery. The socialization of woman into feminine and passive roles was the societal mechanism for continuing the Feminine Mystery. As Beauvoir asserted, "One is not born, but rather becomes, a woman."[24] "It is civilization as a whole that produces this creature, intermediate between male and eunuch, which is described as feminine."[25] Woman's preponderate characteristic, assimilated throughout her life from society, was passivity.

The societal mechanisms that man constructed to control woman were social roles. While Sartre did not specify social roles as the mechanisms for the Being-For-itself to control the Other, he did conclude, "We wish people to conform to the descriptions we give of them."[26] In Beauvoir's analysis of woman as Other, these descriptions assumed the form of roles and myth. The roles that man defined for woman as Other—mother and wife—denied woman subjectivity and freedom. Not only did they define woman's social position within society but also her modes of behavior. They established, in other words, the Sartrian situations within which woman must exercise her power to choose. But, as Beauvoir concluded, the situations, or circumstances, for woman were so confining that she actually was not permitted freedom of choice.[27]

Woman's socialization into passive and feminine roles was neither quick nor easy. It was a process which occurred in stages that reflected woman's biological development. The first stage was a young girl's recognition of her Otherness and, hence, her inferiority. A young girl painfully realized that her inferiority was preordained, a fact of existence over which she had no control.

> The sphere to which she belongs is everywhere enclosed, limited, dominated, by the male universe: high as she may raise herself, far as she may venture, there will always be a ceiling over her head, walls that will block her way. The gods of man are in a sky so distant that in truth, for him, there are no gods: the little girl lives among gods in human guise.[28]

At puberty the young woman entered the second stage of socialization. A young woman's physical changes during this period compelled her to accept and internalize the Otherness that she recognized earlier in life. Now a grown-up, "she cannot become grown-up without accepting her femininity,"[29] with the restricted behavior that it imposed. A girl first perceived her inferiority as deprivation of the worth and freedom of boys. But at puberty deprivation assumed more negative connotations. Woman's inferiority and deprivation became shameful. Being a woman was not only being inferior to man, it was worse.

But interestingly, woman's socialization was not completed with the internalization of passivity and femininity. Woman experienced a third stage of socialization—the crisis of middle age. "Whereas man grows old gradually, woman is suddenly deprived of her femininity; she is still relatively young when she loses the erotic attractiveness and the fertility which, in the view of society and in her own, provide the justification of her existence and her opportunity for happiness."[30] The middle-aged woman, whose social and personal value previously was defined by her reproductive capacity and femininity, thus eventually was denied even these limited estimations of her worth. According to man's definition of her value, the middle-aged woman no longer had social value.

In contemporary society, Beauvoir concluded, the social roles for woman that evolved throughout history finally assumed the form of myth—the myth of femininity or the Feminine Mystery. The myth of woman as Other affected woman as a Being by destroying her consciousness. Woman assumed and believed in her own Otherness. She achieved a state of pure immanence.[31] Woman's Otherness was her self-identity. Woman's Otherness affected her social behavior because she failed to make choices in accordance with her own Being. Situations or circumstances that man defined for her limited her choices. Therefore, woman could not become a Subject, a Being-For-itself, in male-oriented society. As Object, woman lacked the subjective freedom of choice to utilize her own consciousness. She merely fulfilled the roles that man defined for her.

The most common roles for woman in society were marriage and motherhood, both consistent with woman's femininity and passivity. Yet for Beauvoir, the woman who was only wife and mother led an empty and worthless life. The woman who stayed home was doomed to immanence through the continuation of the species and the care of the home. Her own life had no value to her or to society. "Her home is thus her earthly lot, the expression of her social value and of her truest self. Because she *does* nothing, she eagerly seeks self-realization in what she *has*."[32]

But, one might ask, did not woman's role as mother, as trainer of her children, provide some value to her life? Beauvoir did not believe so. The woman who stayed home was a mother in name only. She gave physical life to a child, but she had nothing to give but life. "A mother can have *her* reasons for wanting a child, but she cannot give to *this* independent person, who is to exist tomorrow, his own reasons, his justification, for existence; she engenders him as a product of her generalized body, not of her individualized existence."[33] Beauvoir, however, did not perceive this role of mother as worthless per se. Mothers who worked had more to offer their children. "The woman who enjoys the richest individual life will have the most to give her children and will demand the least from them; she who acquires in effort and struggle a sense of true human values will be best able to bring them up properly."[34] The working mother was, then, another socially accepted role for woman.

But it was a difficult role to play and did not eliminate her inferior condition. The working wife and mother role instead posited new problems for woman. The working woman lacked the freedom to reject or replace those roles that man defined for her. She remained the Other. She remained feminine. At the same time, she developed new professional interests and personal strength. The working woman's unique problem was an intense conflict of roles, or identity crisis. A working woman, by definition, developed an internal conflict between her femininity and her intellectual interests. Because she must continue her image of femininity to appeal to male society, her limited supply of energy rendered a full commitment to a profession impossible. What happened, Beauvoir concluded, was that a professional woman could never be "elegant," which was the epitome of femininity, nor could she be professionally successful. "She is expected to be *also* a *woman*, and she has to add the duties of her professional study to those implied in her femininity."[35]

Other roles for woman also existed in society, but they, too, were based on woman's Otherness. Beauvoir termed these other roles the narcissistic roles of woman. The woman who not only internalized, condoned, utilized, appreciated, or perhaps loved her own femininity and Otherness would develop other roles within society, but still roles condoned by man. Beauvoir discussed the prostitute as the best example of such an alternative role. The prostitute was both the most exploited individual in society and also the individual who exploited the most. Her self-worth was directly related to her femininity, with both measured in economic terms. She was the most exploited individual because her economic existence depended upon self-exploitation of her femininity and Otherness. While the prostitute sold Otherness for profit, she forced the male to worship and pay homage to this Otherness.[36]

Additional roles for woman in society did not necessitate separation from the role of wife and mother, as the prostitute was separate. One such role was that of mystic. A woman in this role was so enamored with life after death and the benevolence of God that she ceased to care about life on earth. She believed that in the eyes of God she was man's equal and that she would find true peace and happiness in heaven. The woman that Beauvoir called mystic devoted her life and being to religion. Religion became the source of all values and personal worth, with worth determined by the strength of one's beliefs. But, as Beauvoir concluded, the mystic "does not escape her subjectivity,"[37] her Otherness. She merely became the object of God instead of man. The mystic acquired no liberty.

The final alternative role that Beauvoir defined was that of the narcissist, a woman who loved her own image. Her Otherness was the only source of identity, and she estimated her own worth through society's reaction to her femininity. She had no personal value or pride, not even in her own femininity. "The narcissist's generosity yields her a profit: better than the mirrors, she sees her double haloed with glory, in the eyes of others."[38] Since the narcissist depended upon the world to determine her worth, she, too, had no liberty.

In summary, for Beauvoir the modern woman was immersed completely in her Otherness, and her character was shaped and defined by male definitions of Otherness and the societal roles it necessitated. Regardless of the specific roles she played in society— mother, wife, worker, prostitute, mystic—woman possessed the same characteristics that controlled her life. She had no sense of self-worth. She failed to develop personal criteria for evaluating her own value and worth. Her importance as a woman, as the Other, was evaluated by those around her. Husbands and children evaluated wife and mother. A working woman both professionally and personally was evaluated by man. The prostitute relied so completely on man's evaluation of her that she staked her economic existence on men she did not know. The mystic turned to God and male-dominated religion for worth; the narcissist relied on public opinion to give value to her life. This, then, was woman's character and human condition in Beauvoir's analysis. Woman was Other. She offered herself to the masculine world for approval. Her life was defined for her and she lacked the ability and incentive to redefine it for herself. "She has been taught to accept masculine authority. So she gives up criticizing, investigating, judging for herself, and leaves all this to the superior caste. Therefore the masculine world seems to her a transcendent reality, as absolute."[39]

Of primary concern for Beauvoir in analyzing woman's societal condition was the quality of woman's existence and how this quality affected woman, not society. Beauvoir assumed, and indeed she proved rightly so, that analyzing woman's status in society without first analyzing her relationship to man was futile. The male-female dichotomy in the world, developed and perpetuated by man, structured society. Society was man-made.

Beauvoir, however, curtailed her analysis of woman's character after evaluating its development and perpetuation. Because woman was so controlled by man and the societal structures he constructed, woman's true character could not be known. Before woman could be herself, society must change to permit her unfettered development. Femininity and passivity must be eliminated by woman becoming a Subject herself. "What is certain is that hitherto woman's possibilities have been suppressed and lost to humanity, and that it is high time she be permitted to take her chances in her own interest and in the interest of all."[40]

Beauvoir's analysis of woman's human and social conditions, woman's lack of freedom to make decisions and control her own life, and her identification of the development and perpetuation of the social roles that perpetuated woman's subjection evolved from her existentialist perspective. Sartrian existentialism denied the possibility of the coexistence of Subjects and Objects within any relationship approximating equality. To maintain its own subjective freedom, the male Being-For-itself must control that which it did not understand and that which threatened its continued existence, namely, woman. Beauvoir reached the same conclusion. "Women, therefore, have never composed a separate group set up *on its own account* over against the male grouping. They have never entered into a direct and autonomous relation with men."[41] She defined woman as Other, an object to be controlled by man so that he may keep his freedom and virility, and she identified the social roles that man constructed and continuously reinforced in order to relegate woman to his definition of her. These Sartrian observations and conclusions were Beauvoir's contribution to the development of feminist ideology. While earlier feminist ideologists sought to describe woman's human and societal conditions, Beauvoir focused on determining their sources and causes.

Although Beauvoir's prescriptions and programs for change reflected no unique contributions to the development of feminist ideology, they still warrant brief mention because they were consistent with her existentialist perspective. Woman must overcome her immanence and develop subjective freedom and consciousness. Once woman achieved personal autonomy, she would experience herself as a Subject, as a Being-For-itself. Yet, Beauvoir concluded, woman could not know what she would be like as a Being-For-itself until she gained her freedom.

How was woman to develop her own sense of personal worth and character? How would she begin to replace passivity and femininity as criteria for self-evaluation? By becoming more involved in the world around her and by assuming roles in society traditionally defined as male, woman would begin to become a Subject. Beauvoir's prescriptions for woman reduced fundamentally to one, woman must seek economic equality. Political equality, in Beauvoir's conception the right to vote and access to the political system, had already failed as tools to improve woman's status and to eliminate her Otherness. Economic independence would eventually destroy woman's Otherness because it would curtail her dependence on man for worth, approval, and existence.

> It is through gainful employment that woman has traversed most of the distance that separated her from the male; and nothing else can guarantee her liberty in practice. Once she ceases to be a parasite, the system based on her dependence crumbles; between her and the universe there is no longer any need for a masculine mediator.[42]

Beauvoir believed that once any woman experienced emancipation, experienced being a Subject instead of an Object, she would strive even harder for total emancipation. Beauvoir considered the intellectual woman closer to emancipation than any woman in the past. Because the intellectual woman realized that she could not go back to being Object after becoming Subject, Beauvoir believed that other women would eventually experience the same phenomenon.[43]

For strategies, Beauvoir merely adopted those of earlier feminist ideologists, which were also consistent with her existentialism. She logically contended that the best method available to woman for achieving the status of Subject was to assume male roles in society, particularly economic roles. For if man in society was a Being-For-itself, then the societal roles, or situations, that he defined for himself must be conducive to his subjective freedom, to his life as a Subject. These strategies, however, were the weakest part of Beauvoir's analysis of woman. Beauvoir first asserted that woman should engage in collective liberation and seek to change herself. Like many of the nineteenth-century ideologists, Beauvoir recognized that

> oppressors cannot be expected to make a move of gratuitous generosity; but at one time the revolt of the oppressed, at another time even the very evolution of the privileged caste itself, creates new situations; thus men have been led, in their own interest, to give partial emancipation to women: but it remains only for women to continue their ascent, and the successes they are obtaining are an encouragement for them to do so. It seems almost certain that sooner or later they will arrive at complete economic and social equality, which will bring about an inner metamorphosis.[44]

The second strategy that Beauvoir described was a socialist transformation of society. In the modern world, not even complete economic equality would transform woman completely into a Subject. All workers were Objects, and all were exploited. For woman to achieve complete emancipation in the final analysis, the structure of society that men had built must also be destroyed. "Working today is not liberty. Only in a socialist world would woman by the one attain the other."[45]

Beauvoir's dual strategies of woman's self-emancipation and the socialist transformation of society, in retrospect, were extremely problematic. When Beauvoir advocated woman's responsibility for her own metamorphosis, she appeared to ignore many of the analyses that she had made earlier in *The Second Sex*. Specifically, she ignored the problem of how a woman who was completely the Other, for example the wife and mother, would overcome her Otherness to enter the marketplace. Second, she also ignored her earlier discussion of the woman who attempted to combine a profession with Otherness and faced a painful conflict between the roles of femininity and professional. Yet, in defining her program for self-emancipation, Beauvoir provided no guidelines to aid woman in resolving this conflict in favor of professionalism.

How could a woman reject her femininity in the modern world? Could she separate herself from the values and mores of society and live as an "island"? These are the kinds of questions surrounding self-emancipation that Beauvoir failed to consider or even mention. It is very unlikely that all women would decide simultaneously to emancipate themselves. Yet this would be the only condition under which woman could separate herself from the values and recognition of male society. Only simultaneous emancipation for all women would provide enough reinforcement for woman to undergo a complete change in self-identity without the approval or cooperation of male society.

In prescribing a socialist transformation of society, Beauvoir encountered the same difficulties that nineteenth-century feminists found prior to the woman's suffrage movement: Who would transform society? Men had created the society that existed. It would be improbable that they would change it. And if men did decide to create a socialist world, would they create an equal place for woman? Does a change in societal structure necessitate a change in man's perspective of woman as Other? Beauvoir, again, did not discuss these issues in *The Second Sex*. While a socialist society may indeed be a prerequisite for complete female emancipation, Beauvoir failed to identify and deliberate on the problems inherent in instituting that society.

Simone de Beauvoir, in summary, offered a cogent and detailed historical, philosophical, and, at times, social scientific analysis of woman's condition. Among her predecessors only Margaret Fuller developed a comparably sophisticated description of woman's societal condition and the social and psychological forces that determined that condition. Yet Beauvoir, much like Fuller, was unable to offer any realistic, clearly delineated program for emancipating woman. She contended that woman must become Subject, but she failed to recommend concrete proposals for altering society. Above all, she completely ignored a discussion of how men might react to these changes, and how their perspectives of woman as feminine and passive might be changed. Yet shouldn't we expect a discussion of these issues from Beauvoir, given her detailed analysis of man's status as Subject and his definition and perception of woman as Other?

Beauvoir was the final feminist ideologist to make important contributions to the development of feminist ideology. Her feminist ideology, and in particular her contributions to its development, were part of the ideological perspective that she brought to her analysis of woman. In Beauvoir's case, this perspective was existentialism. Simone de Beauvoir's most important contribution was her interpretation of the ways in which woman had arrived at the societal condition described by the eighteenth- and nineteenth-century feminists.

THE FEMININE MYSTIQUE

Almost fifteen years elapsed between the publication of *The Second Sex* and the next major treatise on woman's condition. While Beauvoir wrote in France, the resurgence of interest in feminist questions began in the United States. This resurgence, as we have seen, began with Betty Friedan's *The Feminine Mystique* in 1963. Since 1963, many feminist works have been published by and about women. But when we compare the thought of these later feminists to *The Second Sex*, these "classic" works of the contemporary feminists are little more than elaborations and clarifications of Beauvoir's thought. In *The Feminine Mystique*, for example, Betty Friedan developed an analysis of the impact of the feminine mystique on woman. Friedan's analysis was basically the application of Beauvoir's thought to American society of the 1950s.

Friedan began her analysis with a definition of the "feminine mystique" which said "that the highest values and the only commitment for women is the fulfillment of their own femininity."[46] Woman's new feminine role was that of housewife, a role that was considered separate from man's roles in society but nonetheless equal—a role that developed in Depression America of the 1930s. This concept of the feminine mystique can be interpreted as a redefinition of Beauvoir's Feminine Mystery. For Beauvoir, the Feminine Mystery was woman's internalization of her Otherness, a recognition that she was separate and different from man. Her separateness necessitated unique roles, particularly those of wife and mother, to which woman's passive and feminine character was best suited. Beauvoir, however, placed the evolution of the Feminine Mystery at a much earlier time in history than Friedan. Friedan saw it as a product of the twentieth century.[47] Beauvoir, on the other hand, located the source of the Feminine Mystery in the beginning of bourgeois society. Certainly Wollstonecraft's criticisms of the wife and mother role substantiates the fact that the feminine mystique existed prior to the 1930s.

Friedan might counter this criticism by saying that her definition implied that contemporary women and men consider the housewife role as separate but *equal* to man's roles in society. Woman in the past thought of herself as less than equal, and in reality she was. She lacked the political, economic, and legal rights of man. But here Friedan would encounter an analytical problem. She claimed that the modern role of housewife differed from that in the past because modern woman possessed political, legal, and educational equality.[48] In making this claim, Friedan transferred this objective equality to social roles. Male and female roles were equal, she concluded, because woman had equal rights. The objective fact of equal rights, however, did not necessarily admit of subjective equality of roles as she asserted. If woman's role was in reality separate but equal to man's roles, this implied that the role had the same value and worth to society, judged by society's standards, as man's roles. The value of a role (a subjective evaluation) had nothing to do with objective equal rights in society. If this was the case and Friedan was talking about role equality, then Friedan's discussion of the role of housewife did not differ from that of Beauvoir, Wollstonecraft, or other earlier feminists. Since the development of the housewife role, men have always claimed its separateness yet equality to their own roles.

Friedan's analysis of woman's condition abounded with other similarities to Beauvoir's analysis. Friedan asserted, as did Beauvoir, that the mystique encouraged woman to ignore the question of her own identity.[49] Woman's identity was determined by man. Friedan also claimed that woman had a public, not a private, image of herself.[50] Beauvoir had investigated the same idea when she discussed woman's narcissistic nature.

Friedan additionally claimed that "our culture does not permit women to accept or gratify their basic need to grow and fulfill their potentialities as human beings."[51] This argument was the basic idea of woman as Other. Woman, the Object, did not develop her own identity or pursue her development as a human being. She lived in man's image of her and the roles he defined for her. Woman as Subject, the emancipated woman, would be free to develop her potential as a human being. For both Friedan and Beauvoir, the woman who developed her own potential would be the best mother. The woman who possessed no self-identity was a bad mother.[52]

Lastly, Friedan, like Beauvoir, attacked the social sciences and rejected Freud and the Freudians.[53] Freud's concept of penis envy gave validity to male assertions of woman's passivity, femininity, and envy of man. It justified the idea of woman's inferiority.

Thus, when comparing Friedan's and Beauvoir's analyses of woman's condition, few differences in the observations and conclusions they developed about woman's social condition and relationship to man can be found. The only real difference between the two thinkers was the superficiality of Friedan's analysis. Friedan focused on the twentieth century and did not attempt to determine why male and female roles separated in the first place, except to say that Freud and the social sciences influenced the development of the feminine mystique. Yet as other feminists had demonstrated, the feminine mystique as it was defined by Friedan had developed long before social science and Freud. Her methodology also was disturbingly simple. She primarily substantiated her arguments and conclusions with quotations from college friends, other women she interviewed and from women's magazines. But more importantly, Friedan lacked an identifiable theoretical foundation for her conclusions.

Friedan's prescriptions for changing woman's condition and her development of strategies to achieve change were unique, but at the same time they were even weaker than those of Beauvoir. Friedan simply prescribed that woman must say "no" to the feminine mystique.[54] In doing so, unfortunately, Friedan failed to explain how woman could say "no" if she believed in her role as housewife and did not possess the insight and desire to change. Friedan also recommended that woman should combine marriage and a career. But she never faced the problem of the possible identity crisis (or conflict of roles) that could result if woman tried to reconcile her traditional role as housewife with that of professional.

The only part of *The Feminine Mystique* in which Friedan significantly deviated from Beauvoir's thought was in the strategies for achieving woman's emancipation. "I think that education, and only education, has saved, and can continue to save, American women from the greater dangers of the feminine mystique."[55] According to Friedan, educators of women, particularly at the college level, must assume responsibility to "see to it that women make a lifetime commitment to a field of thought, to work of serious importance to society."[56] Friedan's analysis, however, again had problems. College education in the past and present has been a predominately male profession. Friedan was therefore recommending that male educators should aid in changing the condition of woman, which as an important part of male society they helped to create. Friedan failed to consider the issue of how educators should transform woman, why they should think it their responsibility to do so, and who would change their values and opinions about woman.

Friedan, in conclusion, offered no significant contributions to the theory of the second sex and woman as Other that Beauvoir developed. Friedan's analysis of woman, prescriptions, and strategies were even more limited in scope and depth than those of Beauvoir. She did not develop a theory to explain the origin of the male-female dichotomy in social roles. She totally ignored the male's role in developing this difference, except for Freud, and she failed to understand the strength of the feminine mystique when it was accepted by woman. While *The Feminine Mystique*, therefore, may be considered a "classic" contemporary feminist work, its importance lies solely in its polemicism and incitement to action. Yet, even as a polemical work, Friedan's *The Feminine Mystique* has problems. Should a work whose conclusions are substantially unsupported and in some cases incorrect be lauded as a rallying cry for women and be the only exposure to feminist ideas many women receive? A polemical work need not misrepresent historical fact to be effective.

THE FEMALE EUNUCH

Germaine Greer in *The Female Eunuch* offered a third analysis of woman's status in contemporary society. Her analyses and conclusions about woman's status also further explicated ideas found in *The Second Sex.* Any differences between Greer and Beauvoir were insignificant. They were either differences of opinion about the same phenomena or observations that were irrelevant to Greer's theory and conclusions.

Greer began her study by defining "female eunuch."

> The female's fate is to become deformed and debilitated by the destructive action of energy upon the self, because she is deprived of scope and contacts with external reality upon which to exercise herself . . . when she becomes aware of her sex the pattern has such sufficient force of inertia to prevail over new forms of desire and curiosity. This is the condition which is meant by the term *female eunuch.*[57]

The female thus was focused inward and lacked scope and a recognition of external reality. Her awareness of her sexual self (or inner-directed identity) rendered all externally directed desires and curiosity inert. This description of woman as inner-directed incorporated almost perfectly Beauvoir's description of woman as Other and the internalization of Otherness. Since woman as Other was Object to society's and man's Subject, she was inner-directed. She refrained almost voluntarily from involvement in society because she accepted the differentiation of male and females roles. Even the woman who attempted to combine a career and family was inner-directed. She retained her feminine role and attempted to assimilate it into her other roles in society. A woman with a career created a new feminine role—the feminine woman as professional.

Greer's discussion of woman's status in society continued to be identical to that of Beauvoir. Greer contended that woman could only know her present state, that she could not know what she could become, because of her status as female eunuch.[58] The source of the female eunuch was society's male-female dichotomy.[59] Man's power defined and perpetuated male and female roles. Male power castrated woman. Beauvoir had identified the same phenomena, in particular male creation and continuation of the marriage relationship and societal systems that rendered woman unequal. Because woman was inner-directed, Greer concluded that woman lacked initiative to change, to seek other lifestyles.[60] Beauvoir made the same argument. Woman internalized her Otherness, accepted it, and saw no possibility or reason for change.

When discussing how each woman became a female eunuch, Greer approximated Beauvoir's analysis of woman's socialization. Greer contended that the young girl was socialized into a female role, just as boys were socialized into male roles. The young girl learned her "menial role" in society.[61] At puberty new problems developed for the young woman in contemporary society. Puberty was the time of life in which the young woman "adopts the role of Eunuch."[62] "She has to arrive at the feminine posture of passivity and sexlessness."[63] When a young woman assimilated her "menial role" in society, Greer concluded that she was realizing that her inferiority was preordained, a fact of existence.

After discussing woman's socialization into the female eunuch role, Greer turned to a discussion of the roles that woman actually played in society. She defined two different roles. First, the role of mother was woman's most socially accepted role. But for Greer as for Beauvoir, a woman who was only a mother was a bad mother.[64] Second, Greer's analysis of the career woman was almost identical to Beauvoir's analysis. She perceived the same conflict of roles and the debilitating effects that woman as Other, the female eunuch, had on woman's self-development and self-fulfillment. "The little girl may excel in those kinds of intellectual activity that are called creative, but eventually she either capitulates to her conditioning, or the conflicts become so pressing that her efficiency is hampered."[65]

Greer and Beauvoir obviously possessed very similar analyses of woman's status in society. They both identified woman's unequal position in society as a role accepted by woman herself. The role was woman's Otherness, her femininity and passivity, or woman as female eunuch. They identified the same socialization processes for woman. And both concluded that woman's inferior status in society was due to male imposed and perpetuated male-female role dichotomies. When Greer's analysis of woman's status in society differed from Beauvoir's, these differences were inconsequential. They did not render Greer's basic analysis of woman different from Beauvoir's. They did not invalidate any observations that Beauvoir made, and they did not contribute any unique components to the development of feminist ideology.

The first of these differences was Greer's arguments for female superiority. "There is much evidence that the female is constitutionally stronger than the male."[66] This assertion of female physical superiority was unrelated to Greer's theories about female inequality in society. It was not discussed in relation to woman's status or used as a justification for female equality or dominance.

Second, Greer differed from Beauvoir in her claim that men hated women. "As long as man is at odds with his own sexuality and as long as he keeps woman as a solely sexual creature he will hate her, at least some of the time."[67] Man's hatred of woman was, for Greer, another factor in male suppression of woman. Obviously, Beauvoir's analysis, as well as that of the earlier feminist ideologists, radically differed from this line of thought. For Beauvoir, man established himself as Subject, woman's controller, because of his fear, not hatred, of woman. In the state of nature, man's fear of woman as the human representation of nature incited man to develop and perpetuate different roles for man and woman. In the final analysis, however, whether man's reason for initially differentiating roles for man and woman was fear or hatred was of no importance in the perpetuation of roles. After the initial male-female dichotomy had been drawn in society, for whatever reason, the methods employed for continuing the differences remained the same. The extensive similarity between Beauvoir's and Greer's analyses of woman's social status and its development and perpetuation attest to that fact.

The last important difference between Greer and Beauvoir was the interpretations they offered of woman's alternative roles in society, the roles that developed in addition to the traditional roles of wife and mother and working housewife. Greer and Beauvoir offered very different interpretations of the roles of "rebellion"— roles such as bitch, witch, lesbian, and prostitute. For Greer, "There have always been women who rebelled against their role in society."[68] Such a woman revolted against the limitations of the female's passive roles.[69] She rejected male domination and definition of her. Beauvoir, however, disagreed. The woman who chose alternative roles, roles she created in reaction to the domination of man, was not free. She merely reinforced her Otherness. She gained no power in society in relation to man. She was still unequal. By defining her

Otherness herself, she remained separate and distinct from man. Greer asserted that a woman who defined her own role was free and equal because she decided her own future. But Greer failed to consider both the quality of the role that woman defined, that is, if the role really made her equal and more free in relation to man, or if it simply set her further apart from man, and also the fact that these "rebellious" roles were rebellious because male-controlled society defined them as such.

This divergence between the analyses of Beauvoir and Greer was perhaps the most significant. But these differences did not affect the basic propositions and conclusions of their analyses of woman. Both feminist thinkers realized that the woman who chose other roles was in the minority. The development and evolution of woman's status in society and male domination were only peripherally affected by these alternative roles, if at all.

In the prescriptions for woman's future that Greer developed, she again closely approximated Beauvoir's analysis both in the recommendations she made and the problems inherent in these recommendations. Greer concluded that woman must free herself, or become a Subject. "Womanpower means the self-determination of women, and that means that all the baggage of paternalistic society will have to be thrown overboard."[70] Greer also recognized that woman would confront many difficulties in overcoming her socialization and conditioning. Woman would face a conflict of roles.[71] Finally, both Greer and Beauvoir admitted that the "new sexual" regime as Greer called it, or woman as Subject, could not be described. Since woman always had been controlled by man, woman's true nature could not be known until woman developed in a free, uncontrolled environment. For both thinkers, a socialist state was prerequisite for complete freedom for woman. Unfortunately, Greer like Beauvoir failed to describe how a socialist state could be achieved and how woman would free herself if her subjection was internalized.

In defining programs for implementing change, Greer deviated most substantially from Beauvoir. Beauvoir emphasized the importance of economic change, and this was the reason why she viewed a socialist society, an egalitarian society, as an important precondition for woman's becoming Subject. Greer, in contrast, advocated a socialist society not for its economic freedom but for its social freedom. Although she did not identify it as such, Greer's program was utilitarianism. She concluded, "The chief means of liberating women is replacing compulsiveness and compulsion by the pleasure principle."[72] Reinforce woman's actions with pleasure, and they would make themselves free. Greer specifically advocated that woman must refuse to marry because she saw the roles derivative of marriage as compulsory.[73] Second, woman should organize with others for self-help, and women without children should bargain for equality.[74] Women must also become socialists. They must "reject their role as principal consumers in the capitalist state," because consumerism was compulsion.[75]

In general, for Greer, woman "must recapture her own will and her own goals, and the energy to use them."[76] This was Greer's strategy for woman's self-help. Although this strategy was perhaps more broad-based than Beauvoir's economic strategy, it was no more viable. Greer and Beauvoir both provided no guidelines for determining how woman would overcome her "conditioning." Throughout her work, Greer emphasized how powerful woman's conditioning was and how difficult it was to overcome. "A woman who decides to go her own way," she warned, "will find that her conditioning is ineradicable."[77] Yet her whole strategy for change was woman changing herself. Like Beauvoir's economic strategy, she never discussed how woman would obtain the initiative to want to change, how she could overcome her conditioning, who would implement the socialist society, and how man might try to counteract changes in woman and society.

Thus, Germaine Greer's *The Female Eunuch* offered as little to the development of contemporary feminist thought as Friedan's *The Feminine Mystique*. Greer, like Friedan, merely repeated components of Beauvoir's analyses but without possessing an identifiable underlying value structure to substantiate her analysis. Her predominate goal for woman appeared to be sexual liberation. Yet she never explained why sexual liberation was important. She offered no new insights or conclusions about woman's status in society. Except for its greater emphasis on woman's sexuality, her analyses of woman's status was merely a restatement of the arguments of *The Second Sex*. While Greer's strategies for change differed significantly, they no more contributed to feminist ideology than did those of Friedan and Beauvoir. They belonged to the same category of "wishful thinking," or unsubstantiated recommendations for action, which lacked guidelines for implementation and criteria for evaluating their success.

THE MYTH OF WOMAN

While both Friedan and Greer relied heavily on Beauvoir's thought in developing their analyses without acknowledging their debt, it is interesting to note that the contemporary feminist thinker who most substantially deviated from Beauvoir at the same time acknowledged her debt to Beauvoir and the importance of Beauvoir's analysis. This person was Elizabeth Janeway, and her most important work for this analysis, *Man's World, Woman's Place: A Study in Social Mythology.*

Janeway accepted Beauvoir's definition of woman as Other as "essentially and inescapably different," and her analysis proceeded from this definition.[78] She attempted to attribute this concept of woman's place to social mythology. Janeway thus accepted Beauvoir's conclusions, but proceeded to substantiate them by means of the social sciences. She attempted to delineate the sources, development, and perpetuation of woman's place in society by analyzing woman's roles in society as myth.

Although she utilized a different methodology than Beauvoir, Janeway's contribution to the development of feminist ideology was her further elaboraton and development of Beauvoir's analysis of woman's status. Janeway divided Beauvoir's unilateral role of Other into three separate but interrelated roles for woman. She traced the development of woman's status as myth, much as Beauvoir traced its historical development. She then continued to analyze in much more depth than Beauvoir the social forces that operated to perpetuate woman's place, or Otherness, and especially woman's internalization of Otherness. Lastly, Janeway, reaching conclusions identical to those of Beauvoir, analyzed the roles that woman plays in society today.

Janeway began her analysis of woman's status in society by defining woman's place. " 'Woman's place' is a whole set of traits and attitudes and ways of presenting themselves which we think proper to women, along with the obligations and restrictions that it implies."[79] The traits and attitudes that Janeway identified were the same characteristics that composed Beauvoir's Other. But these traits and characteristics for Janeway took the shape of myth. They were the unconscious assumptions that formed the bases for human thought and action, the *Weltanschauungen*, or perspectives of each individual. They were, to use Beauvoir's words, the internalization of the Other by both man and woman.

Janeway defined the myth of woman's place as follows. "They are demanding that women subordinate themselves and their natural talents to men; . . . Nor can they offer logical reasons for this. . . . Here once again . . . is the old myth of feminine weakness, of woman's incapacity and lack of value compared to the male."[80] Thus, for Janeway as for Beauvoir, society perceived woman as valueless and her femininity as weakness.

But why had this myth continued for over one hundred years, as Janeway stated? Beauvoir's answer was because woman internalized her Otherness and because men feared women. Janeway accepted this analysis and expanded it greatly. The myth of woman's place and the division of the world by sex endured because "in a chaotic and confusing world, they suggest control over life because they promise to explain how the astonishing and menacing events we experience fit together."[81] The myth of woman's place, hence, continued not only because it had been internalized long ago by both men and women but also because it was necessary. The myth of woman helped to organize and explain the world. It provided a focus and stability in the face of changing society. The myth of woman, like all myths, not only shaped attitudes but also influenced behavior in the world.[82] For both man and woman, the myth of woman's place shaped the social roles they played. The roles a woman played in society must be consistent with the myth of her place and nature. The same was true for man.

In discussing woman's social roles, Janeway was the first contemporary feminist thinker to define explicitly what she meant by "role." A role implied a relationship with someone else, a mother to a child, a wife to a husband.[83] The repetitiveness of what a role player did within a relationship established continuity, that is, a role; and a role, both activity and relationship, took place within a social system. It was within the social system that the role was understood by others to allow the role, and hence the value of its player, to be evaluated. Thus, roles were both public and private. "It is not just action, but action-plus-expressive gesture, action undertaken in a way that is understandable to others."[84]

Utilizing this definition of role, Janeway concluded that woman's separate roles themselves created conflict within woman. Woman's roles interchanged, and this produced conflict. Woman's role conflict was consequently responsible for woman's internalization of Otherness, instead of woman's internalized Otherness creating role conflict as Beauvoir claimed.

Janeway argued that the many roles that woman played in society necessarily made woman flexible and adaptable. These characteristics themselves were not detrimental to the development of a strong, assertive character. But, when not buttressed with more stable and aggressive character traits, they could produce weakness, the predominate characteristic of femininity. "The effect of the split in woman's traditional role, then, is to direct women toward flexibility rather than single-mindedness, toward responsiveness, rather than decisiveness, and toward the acceptance of selves they live with as a bit inadequate."[85]

The source of woman's internalized femininity and Otherness was, therefore, the insecurity that woman's role conflict created. Because woman felt a failure and uncertainty in her role behavior, she attributed this failure not to the inherent conflictual nature of the roles she played in society but, instead, to her own shortcomings and limitations. Because she felt herself limited, she accepted her Otherness and refused to try to change her roles in society.[86]

For Janeway, then, woman was socialized into femininity or woman's place through myths that operated in society. Man's image of woman's different place were taught young girls as part of the social myths that shaped the world. This analysis was similar to that of Beauvoir. But the perpetuation of woman's Otherness and the internalization of Otherness, Janeway contended, were only partly due to the socialization of man and woman. In particular, the reason why adult women continued the myth of woman's place and accepted their status in society was the development of roles for woman to play in society. The conflicting roles that the myth defined for woman reinforced her Otherness and further internalized woman's sense of ineptness and inferiority.

When Janeway began to delineate the conflicting roles that woman played in society, her analysis drew more closely to Beauvoir's. She identified basically the same social status of woman and the same roles that woman played. Janeway claimed that woman possessed three generally accepted roles in society—mother, wife, and worker.

In discussing woman as mother, Janeway reached the same conclusions that Beauvoir and virtually all earlier feminists reached. Woman's traditional role as mother was still woman's most important duty. Children learned about the world through mothers. Still, Janeway also agreed with Beauvoir's contention that in the contemporary world the woman who stayed home as a mother necessarily would be a bad mother. Society failed to provide any objective criteria for determining the worth, success or failure, or value for the woman at home. Therefore, a woman at home judged the meaningfulness and value of her life only in emotional terms, since her only roles in society were the emotional roles of mother and wife.[87] The only support such a mother could give her children was emotional support; she could not teach them about the world.

Woman's second role for Janeway was woman's evolving economic role. When Beauvoir discussed the professional or working woman, she identified a multitude of conflicts encouraged by woman's attempt to combine her traditional feminine role with a career. Janeway identified the same conflict. A woman who worked and also maintained a home led a "part-time" life. She was neither housewife nor worker, but something in between. Having only a limited amount of energy, a woman must choose between her two roles. One would always be fulfilled inadequately. In Janeway's opinion, the housewife role would predominate as the most important. "For she really doesn't have an equal choice of job first. Our society tells her to put her family first, and any woman who disagrees has got to fight the pattern and face the consequences."[88] Thus, the woman as worker would suffer, and woman's lack of complete success as worker only served to reinforce her feelings of inferiority and Otherness.

In Janeway's analysis, woman's third role was that of wife.

Although the role of wife was closely related to that of mother, it posed unique problems of its own, particularly the fear of competition between man and wife. A woman was always her husband's dependent, even if she worked outside the home. As Beauvoir concluded, a woman's husband and children determined her personal and societal value. Janeway envisaged the wife as the "guardian of emotions" of her husband, not his equal.[89] If woman had power in the marriage relationship, it was the private power that functioned in secret from the world. While she had power over her husband and the emotional relationship of their marriage, woman related to society only through the public power of her husband, not on her own. Woman sacrificed social power for private power in the home.[90] This life of sacrifice and social worthlessness that Janeway described for the married woman was the life of immanence of the wife described by Beauvoir. Woman lacked both social power and societal criteria for evaluating her worth.

When Janeway analyzed the negative roles of woman, the socially unacceptable roles, she identified the same relationship between woman's traditional roles and negative roles that Beauvoir discussed as the narcissist, mystic, and so forth Sometimes, Janeway argued, a woman adopted a role, such as bitch, that on the surface appeared unique. It was separate from woman's traditional roles defined by male society. However, Janeway refuted Greer's supposition that the negative roles evolved from woman's newly found freedom. Janeway instead agreed with Beauvoir that woman's negative roles were merely another form of her traditional place, or Otherness. The negative role encompassed the same traits of inferiority, separateness, and lack of value as the traditional roles.[91]

Thus, Elizabeth Janeway, while proceeding from an entirely different perspective and with a different methodology than Beauvoir, developed an analysis of woman's status in society almost identical to Beauvoir's analysis. Janeway's theory about woman, unlike the polemical works of Friedan and Greer, added significantly to Beauvoir's analysis of woman's status in society in several different ways. By using the framework of mythic thinking, Janeway identified more completely than Beauvoir the social forces that perpetuated woman's status. Janeway also isolated an additional important factor in the continuation of woman's Otherness. She concluded that not only did society socialize young women into Otherness and the internalization of Otherness, but also that the very role structure of society defined for woman supported her Otherness. The conflict evolving from woman's roles in society reinforced and substantiated woman's belief in her own Otherness by formulating a social condition in which woman must fail. Consequently, not only was woman socialized into her inferiority, but her inferiority was constantly reinforced by her performance in society. Success was impossible for woman because failure was built into the social system itself. This one significant difference between Janeway and Beauvoir contributed much to the understanding of the perpetuation and internalization of woman's Otherness and was a unique contribution to the development of feminist ideology.

After her very extensive analysis of woman's status in society, Janeway unfortunately failed to develop any consistent set of prescriptions for woman's future roles and programs for implementing prescriptions. Perhaps inherent in her analysis was that she wanted equality and freedom for woman. Still, she simply prescribed that woman must have the freedom to control her own life. "Women who are doing what they choose to do, whether it is working or whether it is staying home are happier than those who don't have the choice."[92] Perhaps this one sentence said it all for Janeway. Happiness and freedom of choice were prescriptions in themselves.

For concrete prescriptions, Janeway, like Beauvoir, opted for economic change, concluding that the emphasis of earlier feminists on political power did not accomplish any extensive changes in woman's social condition. Economic equality was vital not only to make woman objectively equal to man, but also to give woman's life meaning. For, like Beauvoir, Janeway was convinced that woman must discover some objective criteria for evaluating her own worth.

With the definition of economic equality as the means for changing society and woman's status, Janeway completed her prescriptions and programs for change. She failed to develop strategies and prescriptions even as limited as Beauvoir's recommendations for a socialist society, self-help, and collective liberation. Because of this lack of prescriptions and programs in *Man's World, Woman's Place*, Janeway's contributions cannot be classified as feminist ideology per se, although she made a significant contribution to its development.

CONCLUSION

Simone de Beauvoir's *The Second Sex* has been the only treatise on woman since World War II that may be classified as feminist ideology. Not only was it ideology, but it also contributed significantly to the development of feminist ideology. Beauvoir's concern for the individual development of woman and the value structure that supported her analysis approximated Margaret Fuller's Transcendentalist analysis of woman more than that of any other feminist of the nineteenth or twentieth century.

In *The Second Sex*, Beauvoir began with a statement of her *Weltanschauung*, existentialist philosophy, and emphasized the importance of defining for the reader the value system she employed in her analysis of woman. Of primary importance for Beauvoir, as for all existentialists, was the transcendence of the individual. The existentialist ideal was for the individual to be a Subject, to have control over his or her own life, to be creative, and to have the ability to transcend the limitations of biological existence. In her analysis of woman's status in society, Beauvoir compared woman's societal roles to the ideal of the human being as Subject, and she found woman's quality of life totally lacking in contemporary society. In Beauvoir's interpretation, woman had never been Subject, but instead always had been relegated by man and the society he created to the status of Object, the Other, in the male-defined world.

During her investigation into woman's status in society, Beauvoir did not focus primarily on woman's economic, educational, political, or social positions with the same intensity that many earlier feminists exhibited. She instead adopted a perspective which, as in Fuller, focused on analyzing woman's human condition. She studied what woman was like as the Other and the quality of woman's life. Then, like all earlier feminist ideologists, she attempted to identify the sources of woman's differences from man, the sources of Otherness. She concluded that man was the cause of woman's unequal status in society. Man oppressed woman initially and perpetuated woman's inferiority.

The analysis of how man oppressed woman that proceeded from Beauvoir's identification of man as the cause of woman's Otherness was Beauvoir's important contribution to the evolution of feminism as an ideology. For, while the nineteenth-century feminists cited man as responsible for woman's inferiority, they lacked either the skill or the insight to explain why man initially oppressed woman and to delineate the forces in man, woman, and society that continued the oppression through the ages. Using existentialist philosophy and the social sciences, Beauvoir undertook this analysis.

Beauvoir identified man's initial subjection of woman in the state of nature. When man first began to control nature, man initiated his subjection of woman. Woman represented nature. She was the giver of life and within this physical function man found the mysteries of nature. Therefore, man feared woman as he feared nature. When man learned to control the fears that confronted him, he established woman's position as Other by developing social roles and patterns of behavior for woman that controlled her. He made her Other, and perpetuated her Otherness through a socialization process that began at birth.

Man continued to control woman by developing social roles that reinforced her status as Other. This Otherness for Beauvoir was accepted and internalized by woman herself. This Otherness was the source of all social roles for woman—economic, political, social— that other feminists studied. Woman so internalized her Otherness that she was complacent with her roles. Even if she constructed a new role for herself, such as the mystic or prostitute, these roles were also Other or Object roles. The value of this analysis of woman was that it was the first time a feminist ideologist had attempted to identify the sources and perpetuation of man's control over woman. The only other feminist thinker who investigated this issue was Janeway.

The prescriptions and programs that Beauvoir developed for changing woman's place in society, while they were part of her ideology, did not further the development of feminism as ideology. Beauvoir merely reiterated many recommendations made by earlier feminists in the nineteenth century, although she remained closer to Fuller's analysis than to any other feminist ideologist. Beauvoir prescribed that fundamentally woman must become a Subject. She must realize her potential by eliminating all male and female role differentiations. These prescriptions were precisely those that Fuller made utilizing the ideals of Transcendentalism.

Beauvoir also recommended both short- and long-term courses of action for implementing these prescriptions. First, she advocated self-emancipation for woman concluding, as had many feminists before her, that man, who subjugated woman for centuries, could not be the primary agent for equalizing woman's status in society. Woman's emancipation should begin with economic equality and with woman assimilating traditional male economic roles in society. In the long run, to really become equal woman should work to institute a socialist society. For only in a socialist society where no one was exploited would woman not be exploited. This strategy was, of course, identical to that offered by the nineteenth-century feminist ideologists with socialist perspectives.

In *The Second Sex*, therefore, may be found the only contemporary addition to feminist ideology. It is interesting to note that such proponents of the contemporary feminist movement as Friedan and Greer failed to acknowledge the importance of Beauvoir and *The Second Sex* in their attempts to define a theory of feminism. Perhaps this was because Beauvoir was French and they viewed modern feminism as indigenous to the United States. Or, perhaps they feared that if they acknowledged her work too eloquently, the poverty of their own works would be too obvious.

Still, feminists of the 1960s and 1970s have not contributed to the development of feminist ideology. Friedan's *The Feminine Mystique*, usually credited with beginning contemporary feminism, was too descriptive to be classified as any kind of analytical thinking. Greer, Firestone, and many others were far too polemical and narrow in their analyses of woman. They basically argued that sexual freedom—to have affairs, to be lesbians—was the basis of equality. Other treatises on woman, as discussed previously, were too limited to the methodologies of the social sciences or to one aspect of woman's status, such as legal or economic, to be ideology. But the one outstanding problem with virtually all contemporary treatises on woman, despite their popularity or sophistication, was their lack of an underlying identifiable value structure. Without some underlying set of values, be they democratic, existentialist, socialist, or whatever, it is impossible to have an ideology. Values are necessary to evaluate the internal consistency of any ideology and the efficacy of prescriptions, goals, and especially programs.

These contemporary feminists undoubtedly possessed a set of values upon which they built their analyses of woman. But before the contemporary women's movement can produce its own ideology or even build upon the ideology that developed in the nineteenth century, it must recognize the importance of defining values first. Reading any contemporary work on woman today is a tedious process. The reader may agree with conclusions these feminists reach but cannot evaluate their validity and viability. They incite an emotional reaction instead of an intellectual understanding of the arguments made. To develop a feminist ideology, the contemporary feminists must continually analyze why woman should be equal and how she may become equal in addition to how she is unequal. Only through a continuing analysis of woman's right and need for equality will a feminist ideology evolve from the contemporary women's movement. To date, Simone de Beauvoir's *The Second Sex* has developed the only feminist ideology of the post-World War II period. Other feminist thinkers have only repeated her observations and conclusions in much less substantial, comprehensive, and viable analyses.

NOTES

1. Germaine Greer, *The Female Eunuch* (New York: Bantam Books, 1972), p. 314.

2. Judith Hole and Ellen Levine, *Rebirth of Feminism* (New York: Quadrangle Books, 1971), p. 169.

3. Elizabeth Janeway, *Man's World, Woman's Place: A Study in Social Mythology* (New York: Delta Books, 1971), p. 229.

4. An example of action-oriented analyses is Juliet Mitchell, *Woman's Estate* (New York: Pantheon, 1972). This work places the existing women's movement in a Marxist context to justify it.

5. Simone de Beauvoir, *The Second Sex*, trans. and ed. H.M. Parshley (New York: Bantam Books, 1952), pp. 54-55.

6. Ibid., p. xxvii.

7. Jean-Paul Sartre, *Existentialism*, trans. Bernard Frechtman (New York: Philosophical Library, 1947), p. 18.

8. Mary Warnock, *Existentialism* (London: Oxford University Press, 1970), p. 121, summarizing Sartre's position on man's relationship to circumstances.

9. Sartre, quoted in Ibid., p. 115.

10. Jean-Paul Sartre, *Being and Nothingness*, trans. Hazel E. Barnes (New York: The Citadel Press, 1956), part 3, chap. 1, section 4.

11. Ernst Breisach, *Introduction to Modern Existentialism* (New York: Grove Press, 1962), p. 104.

12. Sartre, *Existentialism*, pp. 37-38.

13. Janeway, *Man's World*, p. 108.

14. Beauvoir, *Second Sex*, p. 38.

15. Ibid., p. 44.

16. Ibid., p. 73.

17. Ibid., p. 59.

18. Ibid., p. 73.

19. Ibid., p. 98.

20. Ibid., p. 128.

21. Ibid., p. 133.

22. Ibid., p. 237.

23. Ibid., p. 243.

24. Ibid., p. 249.

25. Ibid.

26. Warnock, *Existentialism*, p. 116.

27. Beauvoir, *Second Sex*, p. 261.

28. Ibid., p. 278.

29. Ibid., p. 306.

30. Ibid., p. 541.

31. Ibid., p. 243.

32. Ibid., p. 425.

33. Ibid., p. 468.

34. Ibid., p. 495.

35. Ibid., p. 312.

36. Ibid., p. 541.

37. Ibid., p. 638.

38. Ibid., p. 597.

39. Ibid., pp. 564-65.

40. Ibid., p. 673.

41. Ibid., p. 68.

42. Ibid., p. 639.

43. Ibid., p. 644.
44. Ibid., p. 686.
45. Ibid., pp. 639-40.
46. Betty Friedan, *The Feminine Mystique* (New York: W.W. Norton and Company, 1963), p. 43.
47. Ibid., p. 61.
48. Ibid., p. 71.
49. Ibid., p. 75.
50. Ibid., p. 77.
51. Ibid., p. 290.
52. Ibid., p. 119.
53. Ibid., p. 351.
54. Ibid., p. 342.
55. Ibid., p. 357.
56. Ibid., p. 366.
57. Greer, *Eunuch,* pp. 65-66.
58. Ibid., p. 4.
59. Ibid., p. 7.
60. Ibid., p. 64.
61. Ibid., p. 74.
62. Ibid., p. 87.
63. Ibid., p. 84.
64. Ibid., p. 62.
65. Ibid., p. 104.
66. Ibid., p. 19.
67. Ibid., p. 268.
68. Ibid., p. 310.
69. Ibid., p. 311.
70. Ibid., p. 119.
71. Ibid., p. 163.
72. Ibid., p. 347.
73. Ibid., p. 340.
74. Ibid.
75. Ibid., p. 345.
76. Ibid., p. 344.
77. Ibid., p. 153.
78. Janeway, *Man's World*, p. 9.
79. Ibid., pp. 46-47.
80. Ibid., p. 8.
81. Ibid., p. 34.
82. Ibid., p. 70.

83. Ibid., p. 72.
84. Ibid., p. 86.
85. Ibid., p. 100.
86. Ibid., p. 173.
87. Ibid., p. 186.
88. Ibid., p. 196.
89. Ibid., pp. 62-63.
90. Ibid., p. 129.
91. Ibid., p. 245.
92. Ibid.

The Evolution of Feminist Ideology

THE EVOLUTION OF FEMINIST ideology since the end of the eighteenth century has been sporadic at best. The most vital components of feminist ideology had already been delineated by the time Margaret Fuller wrote *Woman in the Nineteenth Century*. Yet it is obvious that feminist ideology is a composite of facets of diverse ideologies. Each feminist ideologist who contributed to feminist ideology derived her analyses of woman and prescriptions and programs for change from the perspectives of other ideologies. The methodologies, values, and criteria used by feminist ideologists to evaluate woman's societal condition were the same methodologies, values, and criteria that ideologists from other traditions employed to critique society in general.

To summarize briefly the major conclusions of the previous chapters, the basic components of feminist ideology evolved from Mary Wollstonecraft's Enlightenment perspective. Wollstonecraft's basic assumptions in the *Vindication* were the Enlightenment beliefs in the rationality, reason, and perfectibility of any human being. She criticized woman's societal condition because woman's irrationality was perpetuated by man-made circumstances and institutions, such as education and religion. Needless to say, the *philosophes* also criticized these same circumstances and institutions for inhibiting the perfection and rationality of man. Wollstonecraft's goals for woman reflected the *philosophes'* goals for man—freedom, rationality, and the development and utilization of an individual's natural faculties.

The utopian socialists Wright and Tristan also contributed to the development of feminist ideology, although their important addition was in constructing prescriptions and programs for changing woman's status, rather than analyzing that status itself. They basically accepted Wollstonecraft's analysis of woman's societal condition adding only a more vehement critique of the detrimental influence of religion on woman, which they derived from utopian socialism. In developing prescriptions and programs for changing woman's status in society, Wright and Tristan applied to woman the recommendations for changing society that the utopian socialists constructed. They prescribed a rational state of society in which woman might become rational. Their strategies were the religious, economic, political, and educational changes of utopian socialism with the ultimate goal of a socialist restructuring of society. For Wright and Tristan concluded that only in a socialist society could woman become rational and equal.

Once the Enlightenment and utopian socialist perspectives of the early feminist thinkers established the descriptive foundations of analyses of woman, the need for a philosophical basis remained. Utilizing her Transcendentalist perspective, Margaret Fuller constructed this basis. Fuller, as the first feminist ideologist, was concerned with identifying woman's true nature, character, and potential. She advocated woman's fulfillment and self-development regardless of woman's nature because each individual possessed the right to be herself. In addition, Fuller suggested that woman must improve herself without the assistance of man since woman's greater intuitive powers rendered her man's superior. These contributions to the development of feminist ideology evolved from an application of her Transcendentalist perspective. Her emphasis on intuition, individual self-realization, and the right that possession of a human soul gave to woman was a Transcendentalist analysis.

Lastly, Simone de Beauvoir in the twentieth century added to feminist ideology an historical dimension to woman's inequality and an identification of its sources and causes in modernity. In *The Second Sex*, Beauvoir constructed a concise existentialist analysis of woman's societal condition. Woman's inferior status in society was derived from her condition of Otherness and the social roles that man developed to restrain her. Beauvoir, like Sartre, emphasized the importance of every individual becoming a Subject, of controlling his or her own life.

The Enlightenment, utopian socialism, Transcendentalism and Existentialism, are the ideological perspectives that influenced the development of feminist ideology. They encouraged women ideologists within each tradition to analyze woman's societal condition. Utilizing the methodologies, values, and goals of their ideological perspectives, the feminist ideologists found solutions to the problems of woman's inequality and the improvement of woman's status in society. Feminist ideology is, therefore, a construct of the important tenets of other ideologies applied to woman. When male radicals criticized society and proposed changes, unusually well-educated women in each radical circle of men applied these critiques and changes to woman's societal condition in particular. The result was that feminist ideology evolved slowly as it emanated from new ideologies surfacing in the Western world.

Analyses of woman's societal condition, prescriptions of goals, and programs for change throughout history consistently preceded feminist activism. Wollstonecraft prescribed an equal education for woman before women demanded a better education. Margaret Fuller advocated equal divorce laws before women asserted their rights in marriage. Beauvoir contended that woman should assume traditionally exclusive male roles in society before women entered the labor force in significant numbers. Thus, feminist ideology did not evolve as part of or in response to a women's movement. Feminist ideology, on the contrary, preceded activism. It outlined goals and strategies for new forms of feminist activism. The source of feminist ideology thus was not woman's (in the generic sense) recognition of the need for change but the insights of innovative and creative women.

In summary, feminist thought is an ideology, one that satisfies a rigid definition of "ideology." Feminist ideology incorporates a depiction of woman's societal condition, an account of the ways in which that condition evolved through history, and an analysis of the male-defined societal structures that have perpetuated woman's inferiority. Further, it recommends prescriptions and programs for changing woman's societal condition, all of which are justified by appeals to the basic values and goals underlying the ideology.

Feminist ideology is, in addition, a consistent ideology in that its values and goals of woman's ideal societal condition form the bases of its critiques of society, prescriptions, and programs.

The contention that feminist ideology satisfies a rigid definition of ideology, however, should not be misconstrued. For it is not meant to imply that feminist ideology is perfect and requires no improvement. Rather, feminist ideology, like any ideology, contains both strengths and weaknesses. Its analyses of woman's societal and human conditions are particularly incisive and cogent. Its prescriptions for changing woman's societal condition are consistent with the moral and human values underlying feminist ideology. But its programs for change are diverse and often too imprecise for practical application. These strengths and weaknesses of feminist ideology, however, are not due to the analytical and creative skills or lack thereof of its authors as is true of many other ideologies. Instead, feminist ideology's strengths and weaknesses emanate from the ideological perspectives of each feminist ideologist who contributed to its development.

In this concluding chapter, these observations about feminist ideology are elaborated upon by developing a brief composite of feminist ideology as it exists today and simultaneously identifying both the ideological origins of each component and the strengths and weaknesses that result from its origins.

FEMINIST IDEOLOGY: AN EVALUATION

One of the greatest strengths of feminist ideology today is its analyses of woman's societal condition. These analyses include: (1) a set of beliefs about how the societal system operates for woman; (2) accounts of woman's relationship to man; and (3) descriptions of both her power within society and her societal roles.

Feminist ideology's description of woman's societal condition incorporates three separate but related components: an analysis of woman's human condition, a description of woman's societal status, and an identification of the causes of both woman's condition and status. Woman's human condition is irrationality; failure to know herself; lack of independence, including psychological, intellectual, moral, and spiritual independence; inability to think for herself, the lack of intellectual abilities, or a sense of self-worth, self-respect, or self-identity.

Feminist ideologists throughout history incrementally identified these characteristics of woman's human condition. Wollstonecraft initiated observations of woman's condition with her Enlightenment conclusion that woman was irrational. Margaret Fuller and Elizabeth Oakes Smith cited woman's lack of psychological, intellectual, moral, and spiritual independence. Wollstonecraft, Wright, Tristan, and the Transcendentalists recognized that woman's inferior social status inhibited the development of her intellectual abilities to the extent that she was unable to think for herself. Because of her inferior intellect, all of the feminist ideologists since Fuller have concluded that woman lacks a sense of self-worth. Beauvoir developed the most recent analysis of woman's human condition with her observation that woman had no self-identity and did not want one because of her internalized Otherness or inferiority.

The causes of woman's inferior human condition were identified when the feminist ideologists throughout history described woman's societal condition. In all areas of life—political, legal, economic, and social—woman possessed an inferior status. Throughout the development of feminist ideology in the nineteenth century, the feminist ideologists expanded the scope of critiques of woman's inferior status. Wollstonecraft identified woman's lack of equal educational opportunities and the subsequent detrimental effect of that lack on woman's human condition. The socialists Wright and Tristan expanded the critique of woman's societal condition to include economic and political equality. Grimké developed the principle of equal pay for equal work, while the Transcendentalists Fuller and Oakes Smith focused on legal rights in marriage as prerequisites for the perfection of woman's intuitive powers.

All of these contributions to the critique of woman's societal condition emanated from the ideological perspectives of the feminist ideologists who developed them. Wollstonecraft's Enlightenment concern with the rationality of woman led her to criticize the educational system that perpetuated woman's irrationality. Wright and Tristan, perceiving that economic and political equality were the most viable alternatives for improving woman's condition, necessarily criticized woman's lack of these rights and equality.

Fuller's and Oakes Smith's Transcendentalist concern for woman's self-improvement, in particular the development of woman's intuitive potential, led to their criticisms of male control of woman executed primarily through the marriage relationship.

For all of the feminist ideologists throughout history, the cause of woman's inferior human condition and societal status was man. Wollstonecraft claimed that man's desire to subjugate woman rendered her inferior. Tristan and Wright identified man-made economic inhibitions on woman as causes of her inequality. The Transcendentalist feminists concluded that man placed woman in a perpetual state of immanence. Grimké attributed the attitude of sexism with subjugating woman, just as attitudinal bias against Negro slaves subjugated Negroes. It was not until the twentieth century, however, and Simone de Beauvoir's *The Second Sex* that the real forces behind woman's inferior human condition and societal status were identified within feminist ideology. Beauvoir, drawing from both an existentialist perspective and the social sciences, delineated the societal roles and social myths that perpetuated woman's inferior condition. She concluded that the Feminine Mystery—the myth that woman is inherently unequal—has permeated society and its history to such an extent that woman believed the myth herself. Woman considered herself unable to compete in the male world. In addition to the Feminine Mystery as a mechanism for reinforcing woman's inferior condition, Beauvoir identified the various social roles that man, as Subject, devised to maintain woman's objectivity or Otherness. The social roles were taught woman through an agonizing three-stage socialization process that included the recognition of Otherness, the internalization of Otherness, and the recognition of a lack of social worth.

Feminist ideology thus possesses a very comprehensive analysis of woman's human condition and societal status, an analysis whose comprehensiveness derives from similarly comprehensive analyses of society within the ideological perspectives of the feminist ideologists. The strength of Enlightenment philosophy was its concern for the rationality and intellectual development of each individual. Hence, Wollstonecraft critiqued woman's irrationality and the educational system that perpetuated it. Tristan and Wright expressed the socialist concern for political and economic equality for all individuals in society. Their criticisms of woman's lack of economic rights reflected this orientation. Fuller and Oakes Smith were concerned about woman as woman and the quality of woman's life, as the Transcendentalists were concerned with the achievement of transcendence for all individuals. Fuller and Oakes Smith concluded that woman possessed greater potential for transcendence, if only male-imposed immanence could be overcome through woman's societal freedom from man. Finally, Beauvoir's existentialism enabled her to identify the social roles that created and continued woman's Otherness.

The prescriptions that the feminist ideologists developed for improving woman's status in society similarly satisfy the requirements of an ideology. After identifying the nature of woman's inequality, the feminist ideologists constructed recommendations for ways to improve society and woman's status that always were consistent with both their concepts of the perfect individual and the values which they originally employed to analyze woman's condition. These prescriptions constructed by the feminist ideologists again emanated from their ideological perspectives.

The first prescription that developed within feminist ideology for improving woman's status was Wollstonecraft's recommendation for equal educational opportunities for woman. Equal education was necessary to achieve her Enlightenment goal of intellectual development and self-realization. Later feminists for whom the same considerations were also important, especially Fuller, elaborated on the necessity of both equal educational opportunities and equal quality of education. As for all Transcendentalists, for Fuller education was the most vital mechanism for each individual to develop his or her potential.

The next prescriptions for changing woman's societal condition evolved almost simultaneously within feminist ideology. They were equality in the marriage relationship and economic, political, and legal equality. Frances Wright, adopting the utopian socialists' perspective on marriage and economics, recommended that woman have equal rights in marriage, including equal property and divorce laws, and equal economic status with man. Recognizing the importance of woman's independence from male control, the Transcendentalists Oakes Smith and Fuller expanded Wright's legal marriage equality to include the concept of marriage contracts and woman's freedom to choose motherhood or not through birth control. In the economic sphere, the Transcendentalists Fuller and Oakes Smith and the Abolitionist Grimké similarly expanded economic equality to include the right to work, the right to equal pay for equal work, and equal employment opportunities because they perceived woman's self-reliance as both a goal in itself and as a means to other goals, such as self-fulfillment and self-identity.

The most important prescription within feminist ideology, however, was not the call for these tangible improvements in woman's societal condition. Rather it was to improve woman's human condition. Both Fuller and Beauvoir (who focused on woman's human condition and quality of life because of their Transcendentalist and existentialist perspectives, respectively) emphasized that woman's most important goal should be her independence from man. Fuller was the first feminist ideologist to advocate woman's total freedom from man regardless of the effects of this freedom on man and society. Woman's human condition demanded independence for its own sake. Fuller, like the Transcendentalists, recommended that woman achieve a state of transcendence (or self-fulfillment) and real and psychological independence from the constraining forces of man and society.

Beauvoir's existentialist contribution to the goal of woman's independence from man was her recognition that woman must free herself. Society and man in the past defined woman as Other. Woman must develop her own personal estimations of worth. She must give her life meaning and her self-identity must evolve from her own evaluations of herself, not those of male-defined society. This prescription of independence was the existentialist concept of Being-For-itself.

In summary, the prescriptive components of feminist ideology also fulfilled the requirements of a strict definition of ideology. After identifying woman's societal and human conditions and their sources in male-defined society, the feminist ideologists devised changes for society that would ameliorate woman's inferiority. Where woman was unequal, they prescribed equality. Where she was constrained, they prescribed freedom. As with their analyses of woman in society, in developing prescriptions the feminist ideologists drew upon their ideological perspectives. Those feminist ideologists who were primarily concerned with woman's societal condition because the perspectives they brought to their analyses of woman were similarly concerned constructed prescriptions that would equalize woman's societal condition. Wright and Tristan fell into this category. The ideologists whose perspectives emphasized the quality of life, such as Fuller's transcendentalism and Beauvoir's existentialism, developed prescriptions that would improve woman's human condition. Thus, the ideological perspectives of the feminist ideologists included prescriptions for either societal change or individual human change, as did the prescriptions they developed for woman's particular status in society.

Both the analyses of woman and the prescriptions for change that the feminist ideologists developed are strengths of feminist ideology because of their consistency and comprehensiveness. The programs for implementing these prescriptions, however, were very weak, even though they satisfied the requirements of an ideology as satisfactorily as the programs of most other ideologies. The reasons for the weakness of feminist ideology's programs were several, and they all derived from the ideological perspectives that the feminists brought to their analyses of woman. First, the programs were weak because they were unsuccessful to the extent that the feminists defined success as complete, de facto equality for woman. While some of the programs improved woman's status, none resulted in complete equality or self-realization.

Second, the weaknesses of the programs in part were due to their diversity throughout history. The analyses of society and prescriptions for change that feminists constructed evolved incrementally. Each feminist elaborated upon and contributed to the thought of earlier feminists. The programs for change in feminist ideology, however, evolved cyclically and depended upon the perspectives of their authors. For example, Wollstonecraft and Fuller viewed equal education as the best program. Tristan, Wright, and Beauvoir conceived of socialism as the only way to equalize woman's condition. Oakes Smith and the suffragists like Spencer concluded that political action was the only viable means for achieving equality. Because there has been such difference in programs, no single program has been clearly developed or continuously updated in view of changing environmental conditions.

Last, the programs may be termed weak because the ideological traditions from which they were drawn failed in their attempts to improve man's societal and human condition by implementing these programs. The Enlightenment, through education and a religion of humanity, did not make society rational. It is therefore not surprising that Wollstonecraft's prescription for equal education, which woman possesses now, has not resulted in woman's rationality. Utopian socialism failed to restructure society along socialist lines and to create economic and political equality for all. Wright's and Tristan's recommendations for economic equality for woman through a socialist restructuring of society therefore also failed because no socialist restructuring of society has occurred.

Fuller's emphasis on equal educational opportunities to develop woman's intuitive powers and intellect also was bound to fail. The Transcendentalists like Emerson sought to make individuals truly self-reliant and self-realized, but the Transcendentalists' goals were not realized. Today more than ever the individual is integrally linked to society. Fuller's strategy of education rendering woman self-reliant and independent, therefore, could not be successful. After she is educated, woman still must rely upon male-controlled society for sustenance.

The political activists also failed to equalize woman's condition. As American blacks have painfully learned, political and legal equality do not necessarily result in societal equality in general. The right to vote and equality before the law have not created equality with white males for either women or blacks. Nonetheless, this political strategy is still regarded as vital today by many feminists, as support of the Equal Rights Amendment demonstrates.

The last program to develop within feminist ideology reverted back to one of the earliest: socialism. Simone de Beauvoir emphasized the obvious fact that political equality had not resulted in societal and human equality. Yet her strategy of economic equality through socialism also was doomed to failure. Beauvoir advocated that woman should assume the economic roles (which by definition are subjective roles) of men in society, if she wanted to become a Subject. By living a man's life, woman might become Subject, especially in a socialist society where no individual was exploited. Yet today woman is free to participate in virtually all economic roles that man participates in, recognizing of course that entry into some of these roles necessitates an initial struggle. Economic equality, the Equal Opportunity Employment Act, and Affirmative Action programs in the United States, however, have not rendered woman completely equal to man. Beauvoir's economic program appears as doomed to failure as the programs of the earlier feminist ideologists.

To date, feminist ideology has not had a successful program for achieving woman's equality. This is not to say that feminist ideology's programs have not satisfied the requirements of a rigid definition of ideology. They have. Its programs have been consistent with its prescriptions and goals. For example, when the criticism of woman's societal condition focused on economic inequality, the feminist ideologists recommended some form of economic action or economic restructuring of society to render woman equal. But while many of the programs were feasible and relatively easy to implement—for example, educational equality—they were only partially successful at best. This lack of success of feminist programs can only be due to the ideologies that formed the perspectives of the feminist ideologists. As the programs of these ideologies failed to implement their goals, so they also failed to implement the goals of feminist ideology.

Why did all of these diverse programs fall short of their goals? Beauvoir hinted at the answer to this question for the programs of feminist ideology. She failed, however, to develop her analysis completely enough to provide a practically useful solution to the problem. Beauvoir's concept of the Feminine Mystery, the consequence of woman's internalization of her Otherness, hints at a solution. Woman was so well socialized into her role as Object by man and male societal structures that woman's self-identity was Otherness. She believed in her inequality and inferiority and accepted it as her human condition as well as her societal status. Woman's *Weltanschauung* thus incorporated an image of herself as an inferior being.

The reason for the failure of feminist ideology's programs to achieve the goals that the ideologists predicted they would achieve thus was not that the programs were inherently weak. Rather the diverse programs developed by feminist ideologists through history failed to compensate for woman's internalized Otherness or inferiority. That is, all of the programs were based on the assumption that changes in societal structures would inevitably equalize woman's societal position and that woman wished her position equalized. For Wollstonecraft and the utopian socialists Wright and Tristan, the societal changes should be male-initiated. For later feminist ideologists, they should be initiated by woman. Yet none of the feminist ideologists broached the question of which men and women would change society.

If man really perpetuated woman's inferior condition as the feminist ideologists asserted, it would be unlikely that he would restructure society to improve woman's condition without prior, significant attitudinal and perspectival changes. The feminist ideologists did not consider the question of the sources of man's incentive to change woman's condition. Even if man decided that woman should be his equal, however, the likelihood that he would know how to restructure society to improve woman's condition would be very slight. Man was bound by the traditions and perspective that created and perpetuated woman's inferiority.

Similarly, woman herself could not be expected to win her own independence and equality based on the strategies that the feminist ideologists constructed. Bound by her Otherness and the intellectual and motivational restrictions it imposed, it is doubtful that woman would possess the incentive to change her human and societal conditions. The most critical weakness of the programs of feminist ideology was that feminist ideology failed to elucidate or provide guidelines for the initiation of change, woman's initial perception of a desire and necessity for equality, and the most viable means to achieve it. This was the logical problem of the programs developed throughout history by the feminist ideologists. Who in society possessed the independence from tradition to begin the process of restructuring society to improve woman's condition if all in society (men and women alike) were bound to a perspective that conceived of woman as unequal?

This failure of feminist ideology to consider the logical problem of initiating radical societal change was a problem prevalent in the ideological traditions that gave birth to feminist ideology. The Enlightenment *philosophes*, for instance, developed programs of a religion of humanity and rational education. But these programs did not achieve their goal of a society based on reason because no one could overcome irrationality to devise a truly rational education and religion of humanity. The utopian socialists failed to institute a rational society because their communitarianism and educational systems did not produce rationality. Irrational teachers did not produce rational children. Communitarianism itself does not eliminate self-interest and competition. The Transcendentalists did not abolish immanence in society. The existentialists did not create a society of Beings-For-itself.

It therefore should come as no surprise that feminist ideology has not yet produced a program that overcomes the problem of woman's Otherness or the problem of woman herself. Yet it is a problem that requires solution for the complete equalization of woman's human condition and societal status. Women are not availing themselves of the de jure opportunities that exist in society. The greatest opposition to the Equal Rights Amendment in the United States comes from women who repudiate change and equality.

What programs could develop within feminist ideology to implement its goals and prescriptions and to ameliorate the unequal human and societal condition of woman?

Perhaps nothing can be done except continuation of the piecemeal advances made by women who desire their independence and equality. Woman's societal and human conditions have advanced far beyond those of Wollstonecraft's description in the *Vindication*. Yet while women are still encountering vehement opposition from some men and women, they doggedly persist in their attempts to alter society, find their own identity, and improve their societal position. More and more women are able to overcome their Otherness (or at least control its influence on their lives) and approximate independence.

On the other hand, perhaps feminist ideology inherently possesses a better program for change than all of the ideologies that contributed to its development. For feminist ideology has outlived most of the ideological traditions that gave it birth and contributed to its development. Feminist ideology has assimilated the most enduring components of analyses of society, prescriptions and programs for change of a variety of traditions that later failed themselves. Today, feminist ideology, a product of diverse ideologies, is a viable ideology. Perhaps its composite nature is feminist ideology's real strength as an ideology. Perhaps its most plausible program is its continued utilization of the most successful strategies of other ideologies as they evolve.

THE FUTURE OF FEMINIST IDEOLOGY

To continue to survive as a viable ideology, feminist ideology also must continue to adapt to changing societal environments. This must occur on two fronts. First, perhaps because of its longevity, feminist ideology appears to have fallen into an unfortunate pattern of development. It seems to progress only in periods without feminist activism. Second, feminist ideology, particularly in the United States, has failed to adapt successfully to the cultural and attitudinal changes of the 1970s, especially in its programs. A reevaluation and reorientation of feminist programs are essential for the continued achievement of feminist goals and prescriptions.

Since the beginning of the women's liberation movement in the 1960s, feminist ideology has stagnated. No significant developments have occurred within the ideology, even in its programs, despite the increase of feminist activism. This lull in the development of feminist ideology, however, is not unique. It also occurred in the late nineteenth and early twentieth centuries during the height of the women's suffrage movement. It appears that feminist action has a tendency to replace feminist analytical thinking. This pattern, however, should be broken. It benefits neither feminist ideology nor feminist activism. Especially in the development of programs for change, it would seem preferable for feminist ideology to impose its values and use its analyses of society and prescriptions to give feminist activism direction. Feminist theorizing during periods of feminist activism would provide movements with fresh ideas and incentives and would also insure that actions would be consistent with and promote basic feminist values and long-range goals. Such an alliance of analysis and action would necessitate that feminist leaders remain loyal to their cause and goals, and not become side-stepped by personal fame, wealth, and influence.

A resurgence of feminist ideology at this time in history also must occur because feminist activism seems to have become mis-directed. Feminist activism today has made a one hundred-eighty degree turn from activism supporting the women's suffrage movement, a turn which has resulted in a novel set of problems for feminism and feminist ideology. Specifically, feminist activism at the turn of the century was overly narrow as many contemporary activists have indicated. When the *single* goal of suffrage was achieved, feminist activism ceased. Consequently, implementation of other prescriptions of feminist ideology came to a standstill.

Today the opposite is true. Feminist activists have outlined a plethora of diverse programs and short-term goals. They are waging too many feminist battles on too many fronts without sufficient numbers, morale, or materiel. The source of this diversity lies primarily in the feminists' alignment with movements and causes extraneous to feminism. While the purpose of these alliances was to create allies and bolster numbers of supporters and subsequent political influence, the effect has been a female backlash. Other, less vocal supporters (the female silent majority), whose support is vital for the achievement of particularly long-term feminist goals, have been alienated.

The most important reason why the diversity of programs and allies must be narrowed, however, is because it has undermined feminist ideology itself. The programs of feminist activists are the only mechanisms in society today for implementing the values, goals, and prescriptions of a feminist ideology. The problem is that some programs of contemporary feminist movements often contradict the values and long-range goals of feminist ideology. Affirmative action and preferential treatment programs for women, for example, are based on the principle of "more than equal," not equality. What a woman is called, "Miss," "Mrs.," or "Ms.," is irrelevant and should never have become a feminist controversy and campaign at the expense of alienating some women. What is important is what a woman *is*. The assimilation of the cause of lesbians in many feminist groups is a gross tactical error. It has and will continue to cause a backlash from conservative and religious women who might otherwise support women's equality issues.

What should be done?

It is time for a reevaluation of feminist activism. The criteria employed for this reevaluation should be the values, analyses of society, and prescriptions of feminist ideology. New programs for activism are needed that are closer to the traditional feminist values (especially equality for all women) and more successful at garnering support from women in society at large. Only more moderate, consistent, and better organized programs that further *woman's* issues in general will end the current female backlash against feminist activism. Only then will feminist ideology continue to evolve as an ideology and provide guidelines and incentives for those interested in woman's human condition.

Woman has travelled a long road to come close to equality. More and more women control their own lives, have a sense of who they are, and determine their own destinies. It would be a shame and a crime against all women in history to lose this momentum and to ignore the wisdom and warnings of the women who went before—the feminist ideologists. After all, woman's equality is not a radical or even a liberal cause. It is a human cause. This has been the message of feminist ideology since the era of Mary Wollstonecraft. It is also a message that many feminist activists today seem to have forgotten.

Bibliography

PRIMARY SOURCES

Beard, Mary R. *Woman as a Force in History: A Study in Traditions and Realities*. New York: The Macmillan Company, 1946.

Beauvoir, Simone de. *The Second Sex*. Translated and edited by H.M. Parshley. New York: Bantam Books, 1952.

Bird, Caroline. *Born Female: The High Cost of Keeping Women Down*. New York: David McKay, 1968.

Dall, Caroline H. *The College, The Market, and The Court; or Woman's Relation to Education, Labor and Law*. 1886. Reprint. Boston: Memorial Edition, 1914.

D'Arusmont, Frances Wright. *Life, Letters and Lectures: 1834/1844*. New York: Arno Press, 1972.

_____. *Views of Society and Manners in America; in a Series of Letters From That Country to a Friend in England, During the Years 1818, 1819, and 1820*. London: Longman, Hurst, Rees, Orme, and Brown, 1812.

Firestone, Shulamith. *The Dialectic of Sex: The Case for Feminist Revolution*. New York: William Morrow and Company, Inc., 1970.

Friedan, Betty. *The Feminine Mystique*. New York: W.W. Norton and Company, 1963.

Gilman, Charlotte Perkins. *The Man-Made World or, Our Androcentric Culture*. New York: Charlton Company, 1911.

_____. *Women and Economics: A Study of the Economic Relation Between Men and Women as a Factor in Social Evolution*. Boston: Small, Maynard and Company, 1898.

Godwin, Mary Wollstonecraft. *Posthumous Works of the Author of A Vindication of the Rights of Women*. 1798. Reprint (4 vols. in 2). Clifton, N.J.: Augustus M. Kelley, 1972.

Greer, Germaine. *The Female Eunuch*. New York: Bantam Books, 1972.

Grimké, Angelina Emily. *Letters to Catherine E. Beecher*. Freeport, Me.: Books for Libraries Press, 1971.

Grimké, Sarah. *Letters on the Equality of the Sexes, and the Condition of Woman, Addressed to Mary S. Parker, President of the Boston Female Anti-Slavery Society.* Boston: Isaac Knapp, 1838.

Janeway, Elizabeth. *Man's World, Woman's Place: A Study in Social Mythology.* New York: Delta Books, 1971.

Klein, Viola. *The Feminine Character: History of an Ideology.* New York: International Universities, 1946.

Mill, Harriet Taylor. "Enfranchisement of Women." *Westminister and Foreign Quarterly Review,* July 1851.

Mitchell, Juliet. *Woman's Estate.* New York: Pantheon, 1972.

Oakes Smith, Mrs. E. *Woman and Her Needs.* New York: Fowlers and Wells, 1851.

Ossoli, Margaret Fuller. *Woman in the Nineteenth Century, and Kindred Papers relating to the Sphere, Condition, and Duties of Woman.* Edited by Arthur B. Fuller. Boston: Brown, Taggard, and Chase, 1860.

Sartre, Jean-Paul. *Existentialism.* Translated by Bernard Frechtman. New York: Philosophical Library, 1947.

Spencer, Anna Garlin. *Woman's Share in Social Culture.* New York: Mitchell Kennerley, 1912.

Tristan, Flora. *Promenades dans Londres.* Paris: H.L. Delloye, 1840.

Wollstonecraft, Mary. *An Historical and Moral View of the Origin and Progress of the French Revolution and the Effect it Has Produced in Europe.* 2nd. ed. London: J. Johnson, 1795.

_____. *A Vindication of the Rights of Woman.* 1792. Reprint. New York: W.W. Norton and Company, 1967.

SECONDARY SOURCES

Anthony, Katharine. *Margaret Fuller: A Psychological Biography.* New York: Harcourt, Brace, and Howe, 1920.

Apter, David E. *The Politics of Modernization.* Chicago: University of Chicago Press, 1965.

_____, ed. *Ideology and Discontent.* New York: Free Press, 1964.

Ashford, Douglas E. *Ideology and Participation.* Sage Library of Social Research, vol. 3. Beverly Hills, Ca.: 1972.

Baelen, Jean. *La vie de Flora Tristan: Socialisme et feminisme au 19ᵉ siècle.* Paris: Editions de Seuil, 1972.

Barrett, William. *Irrational Man: A Study in Existential Philosophy.* Garden City, N.Y.: Doubleday & Company, Inc., 1962.

_____. *What is Existentialism?* New York: Grove Press, 1964.

Becker, Carl L. *The Heavenly City of the Eighteenth-Century Philosophers.* New Haven: Yale University Press, 1932.

Beer, Max. *A History of British Socialism.* Vol. 1. London: G. Bell and Sons, Ltd., 1923.

Bell, Daniel. "Ideology and Soviet Politics," *Slavic Review* 24 (1965):604-11. Attack on Patriarchy." *American Political Science Review* 72 (1978):

Bell, Susan, ed. *Women: From the Greeks to the French Revolution.* Belmont, Ca.: Wadsworth, 1973.

Bluhm, William T. *Ideologies and Attitudes: Modern Political Culture.* Englewood Cliffs, N.J.: Prentice-Hall, Inc., 1974.

Breisach, Ernest. *Introduction to Modern Existentialism.* New York: Grove Press, 1962.

Briggs, Asa. *The Age of Improvement, 1783-1867.* London: Longmans Green and Co., 1959.

_____. *The Nineteenth Century.* New York: McGraw-Hill Book Company, 1970.

Brinton, Crane. *English Political Thought in the 19th Century.* London: Benn, 1949.

Butler, Melissa A. "Early Liberal Roots of Feminism: John Locke and the Attack on Patriarchy." *American Political Science Review* 72 (1978): 135-50.

Clark, G. Kitson. *The English Inheritance: An Historical Essay.* London: SMC Press, Ltd., 1950.

Cole, G.D.H. *The History of Socialist Thought.* Vol. 1. London: The Macmillan Company, 1953.

_____. *Robert Owen.* London: Ernest Benn, 1925.

Collins, James. *The Existentialists: A Critical Study.* Chicago: Henry Regnery, 1952.

Connolly, William E. *Political Science and Ideology.* New York: Atherton Press, 1967.

Cox, Richard H., ed. *Ideology, Politics and Political Theory.* Belmont, Ca.: Wadsworth, 1969.

Dall, Caroline H. *Margaret and Her Friends or Ten Conversations with Margaret Fuller upon the Mythology of the Greeks and its Expression in Art.* Boston: Roberts Brothers, 1895.

Deckard, Barbara. *The Women's Movement: Political, Socioeconomic, and Psychological Issues.* New York: Harper & Row, 1975.

Drucker, H.M. *The Political Uses of Ideology.* New York: Barnes and Noble Books, 1974.

Emerson, R.W., et al. *Memoirs of Margaret Fuller Ossoli.* Vols. 1, 2. Boston: Brown, Taggard and Chase, 1860.

Figes, Eva. *Patriarchal Attitudes.* Greenwich, Conn.: Fawcett, 1970.

Friedrich, Carl J. "Ideology in Politics: A Theoretical Comment," *Slavic Review* 24 (1965):612-16.

Frankel, Charles. *The Faith of Reason: The Idea of Progress in the French Enlightenment.* New York: King's Crown Press, 1948.

Gay, Peter. *The Enlightenment: An Interpretation.* Vols. 1, 2. New York: Alfred A. Knopf, 1967.

Goddard, Harold Clarke. *Studies in New England Transcendentalism.* New York: Hillary House, 1960.

Godwin, William. *Memoirs of Mary Wollstonecraft.* Edited by W. Clark Durant. New York: Gordon Press, 1972.

Gornick, Virginia, and Moran, Barbara, eds. *Women in Sexist Society.* New York: Signet, 1971.

Gray, Alexander. *The Socialist Tradition: Moses to Lenin.* New York: Harper & Row, 1968.

Halevy, Elie. *The Growth of Philosophic Radicalism.* New York: Macmillan Company, n.d.

Harrison, J.F.C. *Robert Owen and the Owenites in Britain and America.* London: Routledge and Kegan Paul, 1969.

Hayek, F.A. *John Stuart Mill and Harriet Taylor: Their Friendship and Subsequent Marriage.* London: Routledge and Kegan Paul, 1951.

Hearnshaw, F.J.C. *A Survey of Socialism: Analytical, Historical, and Critical.* London: Macmillan Company, 1928.

Hertzler, Joyce Oramel. *The History of Utopian Thought.* New York: Macmillan Company, 1926.

Hole, Judith, and Levine, Ellen. *Rebirth of Feminism.* New York: Quadrangle Books, 1971.

Ingarden, Roman. *Time and Modes of Being.* Springfield, Ill.: Charles C. Thomas, 1964.

Jansson, Jan Magnus. "The Role of Political Ideologies in Politics," *International Relations* 1(April 1959):529-42.

Kraditor, Aileen. *The Ideas of the Women Suffrage Movement, 1890-1920.* New York: Columbia University Press, 1965.

Lane, Robert E. "The Meaning of Ideology," in *Power, Participation, and Ideology,* edited by Calvin J. Larson and Philo C. Washburn. New York: McKay, 1969.

_____. *Political Ideology.* New York: Free Press, 1962.

Leighton, Walter L. *French Philosophers and New England Transcendentalism.* New York: Greenwood Press, 1968.

Lichtheim, George. "Comments." *Slavic Review* 24 (1965): 604-11.

_____. "The Concept of Ideology." *History and Theory* 4 (1965): 164-70.

_____. *The Concept of Ideology and Other Essays.* New York: Vintage Books, 1967.

_____. *The Origins of Socialism.* New York: Frederick A. Praeger, 1969.

Manuel, Frank E. *Age of Reason.* Ithaca, N.Y.: Cornell University Press, 1959.

_____, ed. *Utopias and Utopian Thought.* Boston: Houghton Mifflin, 1966.

Mark, Max. *Modern Ideologies.* New York: St. Martin's Press, 1973.

Miller, Perry, ed. *The Transcendentalists: An Anthology.* Cambridge: Harvard University Press, 1950.

Morton, A.L. *The English Utopia.* London: Lawrence & Wishart, 1952.

Mullins, William A. "On the Concept of Ideology in Political Science," *American Political Science Review* 66 (June 1972).

Mumford, Lewis. *The Story of Utopias.* New York: Peter Smith, 1922.

Murray, Lewis. *Studies in the English Social and Political Thinkers of the Nineteenth Century.* Vol. 1. Cambridge: W. Heffer and Sons, Ltd., 1929.

Naess, Arne. *Democracy, Ideology and Objectivity—Studies in the Semantics and Cognitive Analysis of Ideological Controversy.* Oxford: Basil Blackwell, 1956.

O'Neill, William L. *Everyone Was Brave: A History of Feminism in America.* Chicago: Quadrangle Books, 1969.

Owen, Robert. *The Book of the New Moral World.* London: The Home Colonization Society, 1842.

_____. *Lectures on an Entire New State of Society.* London: J. Brooks, 1830.

_____. *The Life of Robert Owen, Written by Himself.* London: Frank Cass & Co., Ltd., 1965.

_____. *A New View of Society and Other Writings.* Edited by G.D.H. Cole. London: J.M. Dent & Sons, Ltd., 1927.

_____. *The Revolution in the Mind and Practice of the Human Race.* London: Effingham Wilson, 1869.

Owen, Robert Dale. *Threading My Way.* New York: G.W. Carlton & Company, 1874.

Partridge, P.H. "Politics, Philosophy, Ideology."*Political Studies* 9 (1961): 217-35.

Pierce, Christine. "Natural Law, Language and Women." In *Women in Sexist Society,* edited by Virginia Gornick and Barbara Moran. New York: Signet, 1971, pp. 242-58.

Puech, Jules L. *La vie et l'oeuvre de Flora Tristan, 1803-1844.* Librairie Marcel Rivière et Cie, 1925.

Riegel, Robert E. *American Feminists.* Lawrence; University of Kansas Press, 1963.

Roucek, J.S. "A History of the Concept of Ideology." *Journal of the History of Ideas* 5 (1944).

Sartori, Giovanni, "Politics, Ideology and Belief Systems." *American Political Science Review,* June 1969.

Sartre, Jean-Paul. *Being and Nothingness.* Translated by Hazel E. Barnes. New York: The Citadel Press, 1956.

_____. *Existentialism and Humanism.* Translated by Philip Mairet. London: Methuen, 1948.

Shils, Edward. "The Concept and Function of Ideology." *International Encyclopedia of the Social Sciences* 7 (1974).

Shklar, Judith, ed. *Political Theory and Ideology.* New York: The Macmillan Company, 1966.

Soltan, Roger. *French Political Thought in the Nineteenth Century.* New Haven: Yale University Press, 1931.

Vogel, Stanley. *German Literary Influences on the American Transcendentalists.* New Haven: Yale University Press, 1955.

Warnock, Mary. *Existentialism.* London: Oxford University Press, 1970.

Waterman, William Randall. *Frances Wright.* New York: AMS Press, 1967.

Watson, J. Steven. *The Reign of George III, 1760-1815.* Oxford: Clarendon Press, 1960.

Whicher, George, ed. *The Transcendentalist Revolt Against Materialism.* Boston: D.C. Heath and Company, 1949.

Woodward, Sir Llewellyn. *The Age of Reform, 1815-1870.* 2nd ed. Oxford: Oxford University Press, 1962.

Wyman, Mary Alice, ed. *Selections from the Autobiography of Elizabeth Oakes Smith.* Lewiston, Me.: Lewiston Journal Company, 1924.

_____. *Two American Pioneers: Seba Smith and Elizabeth Oakes Smith.* New York: Columbia University Press, 1927.

Index

About the Author

Judith A. Sabrosky is Visiting Associate Professor of Social Sciences at the United States Military Academy. She is currently writing a book entitled *Military Justice for the 1980s* and coediting an anthology entitled *The Eagle's Brood: American Civil-Military Relations.*